THE MYSTERY OF NAMES

By
Dominic Bayor, MSC

The Mystery Of Names

Copyright © 2025 Dominic Bayor

All rights reserved. This book or any portion thereof may not be reproduced or used in any manner whatsoever without the express written permission of the publisher except for the use of brief quotations in a book review.

Published by: London Book Publisher

Table Of Contents

DEDICATION v

CHAPTER 1 Introduction 1

CHAPTER 2 Names And Destiny: How Do They Influence Our Path? 3

CHAPTER 3 Characters Whose Names Were Changed To Fulfill Their Destiny 6

CHAPTER 4 Soul Names And Their Vibrations: The Male Akan Names 9

CHAPTER 5 The Mystery Of Surnames 17

CHAPTER 6 Good And Bad Names 23

CHAPTER 7 The Power Of Spiritual Identity 29

CHAPTER 8 The Power Of The Name Of Jesus 35

CHAPTER 9 Inheritances In Christ 42

CHAPTER 10 Naming Ceremony 46

CHAPTER 11 The Use Of Spiritual Tokens In Christening Ceremonies 51

CHAPTER 12 The Names Of The Blood 54

CHAPTER 13 In Whose Name Should Believers Pray? 64

CHAPTER 14 Is The Name Of Jesus Absolute? 68

CHAPTER 15 Classical Examples Of Biblical Characters Who Prayed In The Name Of Jesus And Had Their Results................... 72

CHAPTER 16 Requirements For Prayer.. 77

CHAPTER 17 The Identity Of Jesus.. 80

CHAPTER 18 Foundation Of Names: The Twelve Apostles......... 83

CHAPTER 19 Jesus Christ: The Solid Foundation For Building God's People 87

CHAPTER 20 The Attributes Of God... 90

DEDICATION

To My Beloved Mother, Eunice Williams,

This book is dedicated with heartfelt gratitude to you—a woman of unwavering faith, boundless love, and exceptional devotion. You have been the cornerstone of my spiritual formation, instilling in me the values of righteousness, compassion, and steadfast trust in the Lord. Through your nurturing spirit, you have not only shaped my character but also deepened my understanding of who I am in Christ.

Your wisdom and grace have been a constant source of guidance, molding my life through both fervent prayer and consistent example. The foundation on which I stand is built upon the countless prayers you have offered, and your life has revealed to me the profound meaning of both earthly and eternal identity—each intricately crafted by the hand of God.For this enduring gift, I remain eternally grateful.

Your steadfast faith and sacrificial love have left an indelible legacy, one that inspires me daily to walk in obedience and purpose. With grace, patience, and humility, you have illuminated the path of truth and righteousness, setting a standard that continues to shape my life and ministry.

This work stands as a tribute to the extraordinary mother you are and to the immeasurable impact you have had on my life. Your prayers have been my sanctuary, your words a source of strength, and your life a living testimony of Christlike devotion. Though words can never fully express my gratitude, may this dedication serve as a heartfelt tribute to the love, wisdom, and faith you have so generously imparted.

With all my love and deepest gratitude,

Dominic Bayor.

CHAPTER 1
Introduction

Names possess a profound significance that transcends mere designation; they encapsulate identity, purpose, and destiny. In *Genesis 2:19*(NIV), we are presented with a pivotal moment in the creation narrative: *"Now the Lord God had formed out of the ground all the wild animals and all the birds in the sky. He brought them to the man to see what he would name them, and whatever the man called each living creature, that was its name."* This passage underscores the sacred responsibility entrusted to humanity—specifically Adam—to name every living creature. In doing so, Adam was not simply assigning random titles; he was exercising authority and establishing a divinely ordained order. Each name served to articulate the essence and role of the creature within the broader framework of creation. This foundational act reveals that naming is not a superficial task but a means of discerning and articulating the intrinsic nature of a being. In the Hebrew language, the word for "name," שֵׁם(shem), carries a weightier connotation. It encompasses not only a literal designation but also one's essence, character, and reputation. Thus, to name something in the biblical context is to recognize and affirm its identity and function within the divine order. Through this lens, names are deeply intertwined with the destiny and role of individuals or entities, reflecting the purposeful structure of the cosmos.

A compelling example of this principle is found in the naming of Eve. As described in **Genesis 3:20** (NIV): *"Adam named his wife Eve, because she would become the mother of all the living."* The name "Eve" is emblematic of her twofold identity. On one level, she is Adam's companion—his wife. On another, more expansive level, she holds the vital role of being the matriarch of all humanity. Her name encapsulates both relational and generational significance, illustrating how nomenclature in the biblical tradition is intricately connected to divine purpose.

Eve's name, therefore, serves not only as a personal designation but as a revelation of her vocation and spiritual significance. It exemplifies how names, within the biblical worldview, are instruments of meaning that shape one's path and reflect divine intention. Far from being arbitrary, names are woven into the fabric of personal and communal identity, guiding individuals toward their ordained roles within creation.

This exploration into the theology of naming offers a richer understanding of how names function as conduits of purpose and calling. By examining the biblical narrative and linguistic context, we uncover the depth and intentionality with which names are bestowed. In doing so, we gain a greater appreciation for the spiritual and existential weight that names carry, and how they continue to shape identity, influence life trajectories, and reveal the hidden dimensions of our place in the world.

CHAPTER 2
Names And Destiny: How Do They Influence Our Path?

Names carry a profound significance that extends beyond simple designation; they have the capacity to influence the course of an individual's life. In ancient cultures, the act of naming a child was far more than a customary practice—it was regarded as a solemn and spiritual endeavor. Parents approached this task with great care, striving to discern the true name of their child through divine revelation. This process entailed discerning the child's purpose, destiny, and any sacred directives or warnings, including abominations associated with their existence. When such revelations appeared through dreams or visions, parents would consult genuine prophets or seers to verify and understand the messages received. This rigorous inquiry was essential for aligning the child's name with their divine mission, thereby providing clarity about the path they were meant to follow and enabling them to fulfill their unique calling.

In contrast, many individuals today remain unaware of these spiritual dimensions, which often results in lives that feel disconnected from their intended purpose and divine calling. Grasping the deeper meaning behind one's name and its connection to destiny is crucial for harmonizing with God's will. A notable biblical example illustrating this principle is found in the story of Manoah, the father of Samson. In **Judges 13:3-5** (NIV), the angel of the Lord appeared to Manoah's wife, revealing the divine purpose of the child she would bear, thereby establishing his name and mission before birth:

"You will become pregnant and have a son whose head is never to be touched by a razor because the boy is to be a Nazirite, dedicated to God from the womb. He will lead in delivering Israel from the hands of the Philistines." This revelation granted Manoah and his wife profound insight into their son's future role, linking his name intrinsically to his sacred calling.

Similarly, Rebekah's experience further demonstrates the importance of seeking divine guidance regarding destiny. As recorded in **Genesis 25:22–23** (NIV), when the twins within her womb struggled, she sought the Lord's counsel:

"The babies jostled each other within her, and she said, 'Why is this happening to me?' So, she went to inquire of the Lord. The Lord said to her, 'Two nations are in your womb, and two peoples from within you will be separated; one people will be stronger than the other, and the older will serve the younger."

Rebekah's inquiry revealed a profound spiritual truth: she was carrying not just two children, but two nations whose destinies would be defined by conflict and rivalry. The physical struggle she felt was a prophetic indication of the historical tension that would shape generations.Through this divine disclosure, God revealed that the twins would become the progenitors of two distinct nations— Esau(Edom)and Jacob(Israel)—highlighting how names and identities can influence the trajectory of history itself. This narrative demonstrates the profound impact that recognizing spiritual identity and purpose can have, extending beyond the individual to influence entire nations and geopolitical dynamics.

Given these examples, the practice of discerning a child's spiritual identity and divine purpose before naming remains as vital today as it was in biblical times. Such spiritual inquiry offers invaluable insight into the unique paths children are destined to pursue. By seeking divine guidance and revelation, parents can ensure that their children's lives are aligned with God's design, thereby providing them with a clear sense of direction and purpose. Absent this intentional discernment, many children may grow up unaware of their true vocation, vulnerable to the complexities and distractions of life, and disconnected from their divine calling.

In a contemporary context where many seek clarity and meaning, parents bear a profound responsibility to pursue spiritual discernment concerning their children's destinies. Through prayerful reflection and consultation, they can gain understanding of the roles their children are meant to fulfill within God's overarching plan. Just as Rebekah's inquiry influenced the course of nations, parents today have the opportunity to shape the lives of their children by fostering alignment with their divine purpose. The names bestowed, coupled with a deeper comprehension of their significance, are not merely personal; they hold the potential to affect broader communities and history. Embracing this sacred practice equips parents to guide their children toward fulfillment and purpose, setting them firmly on the path intended by God's eternal design.

CHAPTER 3
Characters Whose Names Were Changed To Fulfill Their Destiny

If names were irrelevant and had no impact on our lives, why did God change the names of specific individuals in the Bible? The answer is clear: Names are intricately connected to our identities, purposes, and destinies. God's decision to alter the names of His chosen ones was not merely for the sake of change but was purposeful and strategic, aligning their identities with the roles they were destined to fulfil. Anyone who argues that names do not affect our lives is, at best, unaware of the deeper spiritual realities at play.

One of the most prominent examples of a name change in the Bible is that of Abram, who became Abraham. Hitherto, he was known as Abram, which means "exalted father," but God had a greater destiny for him. In Genesis 17:5 (NIV), God declared, *"No longer will you be called Abram; your name will be Abraham, for I have made you a father of many nations."*

This change was not arbitrary; it stood for God's covenant with Abraham. His new name signified his divine purpose as the father of many nations, marking the fulfillment of God's promise to him. Through this name, Abraham became the patriarch of Israel and the ancestor of countless people, fulfilling God's eternal plan.

Another significant name change is that of Jacob, who became Israel. Hitherto, Jacob, whose name meant "supplanter" or "deceiver," had lived up to that meaning by deceiving his father and brother. However, in Genesis 32:28 (NIV), when Jacob wrestled with the angel, his character was transformed, and his name was changed: ***"Then the man said, 'Your name will no longer be Jacob, but Israel because you have struggled with God and with humans and have overcome.*** *"* This new name, Israel, meaning "he who struggles with God," reflected Jacob's spiritual transformation and his pivotal role in forming the nation of Israel. His destiny was no longer about deceit but about prevailing through faith and becoming the father of a nation God chose.

The third notable example is Saul, who became Paul. Hitherto, Saul was a zealous persecutor of Christians, a man consumed by religious pride and anger. However, on his journey to Damascus, Saul had a life-changing encounter with Jesus Christ. In Acts 9:4-6 (NIV), the Lord confronted Saul, saying, ***"Saul, Saul, why are you persecuting me?"*** After Saul's dramatic conversion, his name was changed to Paul, marking a radical transformation in his life and mission. In Acts 13:9 (NIV), it is written, ***"Then Saul, who was also called Paul, filled with the Holy Spirit, looked straight at Elymas and said...*** *"* The change of name symbolized Saul's transformation in Christ and his divine calling to spread the gospel to the Gentiles. His former identity as a persecutor was left behind, and his new name reflected the purpose and mission God had assigned to him.

These examples prove that names in the Bible are not mere titles but are closely tied to destiny and purpose. God changed the names of Abram, Jacob, and Saul to align their identities with their divine calling. Each name change marked a significant turning point in their lives, signifying a new direction, mission, and destiny they were meant to fulfil on earth. Do not trivialise the significance of names, as their importance carries immense spiritual and practical benefits.

Many people encounter difficulties in life because they do not bear the names ordained for them by God before their arrival on earth. If a prophet, under the guidance of the Holy Spirit, reveals the original name God has given you, it is vital to undergo the proper legal process to formalize the change. Embracing the name God has destined for you is essential to aligning with His divine purpose and fulfilling the unique calling He has placed upon your life.

CHAPTER 4
Soul Names And Their Vibrations: The Male Akan Names

In Ghanaian culture, particularly among the Akan people, the day of the week on which a person is born plays a vital role in shaping their destiny. Each day is associated with a soul name, believed to embody the spiritual energy of that day. These soul names, assigned to individuals based on the day of the week they were born, are not mere titles but are deeply connected to a person's destiny and life purpose. Each name carries unique vibrations that shape the individual's character, behavior, and life experiences. In this chapter, we will explore the Akan soul names, which are assigned based on the days of the week, from Monday to Sunday.

1. Cudjoe (Monday)

The name Cudjoe is given to boys born on Monday. Monday, the first day of the week, is associated with new beginnings, creation, and fresh starts. People born on this day are often considered to be thoughtful, introspective, and emotionally grounded. They are believed to connect strongly to their inner selves. They are seen as reflective individuals seeking to understand life's more profound truths. Cudjoe's energy encourages stability and emotional strength, making these individuals excellent listeners and empathetic companions. People with this name are often calm, measured, and considerate. Their intuition is strong, and they can make wise decisions, particularly when faced with life's challenges. The vibration of Cudjoe is nurturing and supportive, aligning the bearer with spiritual growth and emotional harmony.

2. Kwabena (Tuesday)

Born on Tuesday, Kwabena is a dynamic and energetic individual. Tuesday is associated with Mars, symbolizing action, strength, and willpower. A person named Kwabena is known for courage, ambition, and drive. Kwabena carries the vibration of boldness and action, thriving in environments that require decisiveness and initiative. The energy of Tuesday imbues Kwabena with an unrelenting drive to succeed, often making him highly competitive. Kwabena's vibration is one of strength and resilience. He is energetic and determined, often finding himself at the forefront of any venture he pursues. With a deep sense of justice, Kwabena has an innate desire to fight for what he believes is right, making him a passionate defender of ideals.

3. Kwaku (Wednesday)

Kwaku is the name given to boys born on Wednesday, a day governed by the planet Mercury. This day is often associated with intellect, communication, and adaptability. People born on Wednesday tend to be sharp-witted, articulate, and innovative. Kwaku's vibration embodies mental agility and quick thinking. He often sees things from multiple perspectives and communicates ideas efficiently. Mercury's influence fosters creativity and intellectual curiosity, making Kwaku an excellent problem solver. Kwaku is associated with mental strength, intelligence, and adaptability. Those with this name are quick learners and excel in fields that require communication, such as teaching, writing, or public speaking.

Naturally curious, Kwaku is constantly seeking new knowledge and experiences.

4. Yaw (Thursday)

Yaw, the name for boys born on Thursday, carries the vibration of leadership, authority, and responsibility. Thursday is ruled by the planet Jupiter, which symbolizes expansion, wisdom, and justice. People born on Thursday are wise and confident. The energy of Yaw is expansive and magnanimous. People with this name are often viewed as natural leaders with a deep sense of responsibility. They are drawn to wisdom and philosophy, seeking to make a meaningful impact on the world around them. Their spiritual energy is aligned with growth and prosperity, both material and intellectual. Those named Yaw often have an innate sense of justice and fairness. They are principled and likely to be leaders in their community or profession. Their ability to inspire others and their deep knowledge often make them trusted advisors.

5. Kofi (Friday)

Kofi is the name given to boys born on Friday, a day associated with Venus, the planet of love, beauty, and harmony. People born today are compassionate, artistic, and deeply connected to others. Kofi's vibration is one of love and nurturing. These individuals are naturally compassionate and empathetic, often putting the needs of others before their own. Venus's energy imbues them with a strong appreciation for beauty in art, nature, or relationships. Kofi's vibration is one of harmony and balance. Those with this name are often diplomatic, social, and well-liked by others. They have an innate ability to connect with people deeply and emotionally and are likely to be in careers that involve helping or supporting others.

6. Kwame (Saturday)

Kwame is the name given to boys born on Saturday, a day associated with Saturn, the planet of discipline, structure, and responsibility. People born on Saturday are serious, focused, and highly determined. Kwame's vibration reflects steadfastness and perseverance. Individuals named Kwame are often guided by a deep sense of responsibility, which fuels their dedication to achieving long-term goals. Their commitment to purpose and persistence propels them toward meaningful accomplishments. They tend to be disciplined and adopt a no-nonsense approach to life. Kwame often excels in areas that require hard work, dedication, and organization. He is a practical and reliable individual who tends to succeed in his endeavors due to his commitment and ability to focus on his goals.

7. Akwasi (Sunday)

Akwasi is the name given to boys born on Sunday, a day associated with the Sun. The Sun represents vitality, energy, and leadership. People born on Sunday are typically seen as charismatic, confident, and influential. Akwasi's energy is vital and creative. Those born on Sunday are often natural leaders with a magnetic presence. They are filled with energy and creativity, and their actions are usually driven by a desire to make a difference in the world. The Sun's energy instils a sense of purpose and encourages individuals to shine brightly in their chosen fields. People named Akwasi are often outgoing, ambitious, and have a strong sense of self. They tend to be highly confident and radiate a natural charm that draws others to them. They serve as sources of inspiration and motivation for those around them.

Soul Names And Their Vibrations: The Female Akan Soul Names

1. Adwoa (Monday)

Adwoa is the name given to females born on Monday. The vibration of this name reflects calmness, peace, and gentleness. The day Monday is traditionally associated with the moon, which is connected to nurturing, sensitivity, and emotional depth in many cultures. People with the name Adwoa are often perceived as serene and compassionate. Their presence tends to comfort others and are believed to be natural caregivers. The vibration of Adwoa may also give her a nurturing role in life, both in the family and the community. This name suggests an intuitive and empathetic woman with an innate understanding of people's emotional needs.

2. Abena (Tuesday)

Abena is the Akan name given to females born on Tuesday. The essence of the name Abena is linked with qualities of strength, assertiveness, and leadership, as Tuesday is governed by Mars, the planet of action, energy, and courage. Individuals named Abena are often recognized for their ambition and unwavering determination. They have a spirited nature and a natural drive to take charge. With a passionate sense of purpose, she embodies the energy of action, making these women born leaders, and effective problem solvers. When faced with challenges, she steps up with resilience, offering strength and guidance to any situation. Her inner drive fuels her pursuit of goals with unwavering passion and resolve.

3. Akua (Wednesday)

Akua is the name for females born on Wednesday. This name carries the vibration of intelligence, creativity, and adaptability. Wednesday is associated with Mercury, which governs communication, intellect, and versatility. Women named Akua are gifted in the arts, communication, and other creative fields. They tend to be articulate, thoughtful, and intellectually curious. The vibration of Akua enables her to express herself clearly and persuasively, and she may excel in professions that require creativity and innovation. These women are known for adapting to different situations and making quick decisions. Akua's energy is flexible and resourceful.

4. Yaa (Thursday)

Yaa is the name given to females born on Thursday, a day governed by Jupiter, the planet of growth, expansion, and knowledge. The essence of the name Yaa is connected to wisdom, leadership, and spiritual fortitude. Women named Yaa are often viewed as wise and visionary, with a profound understanding of life. They are naturally drawn to philosophical and spiritual pursuits, seeking deeper truths. The energy of Yaa encourages these women to lead with purpose, inspiring others through their insight and guidance. Yaa is often seen as a grounded figure, offering valuable mentorship, advice, or leadership to those around her. The name embodies a sense of intellectual and spiritual growth, highlighting the potential for expansion in both realms.

5. Afia (Friday)

Afia is the soul name for females born on Friday. The vibration of Afia is deeply connected to beauty, harmony, and creativity.

Friday is associated with Venus, the planet of love, beauty, and aesthetics. Those named Afia are graceful, artistic, and charming. The energy of this name makes these women naturally attuned to beauty and art in all its forms. They have a strong appreciation for the finer things in life, and many of them are drawn to careers in the arts, fashion, or design. The vibration of Afia encourages a life of balance and peace, and these women tend to be loving, kind, and nurturing. Their presence tends to calm and soothe those around them.

6. Ama (Saturday)

Ama is the name given to females born on Saturday. The vibration of this name carries a sense of resilience and practicality—Saturn, the planet of discipline, responsibility, and structure, rules Saturday. People named Ama are often hardworking, practical, and dependable. The vibration of Ama encourages these women to build strong foundations for their lives and to approach challenges with a sense of discipline and focus. They are reliable and responsible individuals with a deep understanding of duty to their families and communities. Ama's energy fosters perseverance and strength, helping her overcome obstacles with determination.

7. Akosua (Sunday)

Akosua is the name given to females born on Sunday. Their vibration is linked to leadership, charisma, and vitality. Sunday is ruled by the sun, a symbol of light, power, and vitality. Akosua people are charismatic, energetic, and full of life. The energy of Akosua empowers these women to stand out and take charge of their circumstances. They are natural leaders and are often the centre of attention in social settings. Akosua's vibration inspires confidence and enthusiasm, helping her to inspire and motivate others. Women with this name are radiant, powerful, and destined for greatness.

The Akan soul names, given to both males and females based on the day of the week a person is born, are far more than mere traditions. They carry potent vibrations that shape an individual's character, personality, and life direction. From Adwoa to Akosua and from Kwadwo or Cudjoe to Akwasi, each name encapsulates the unique spiritual essence of the day it corresponds to. These names are believed to align individuals with their divine destinies, revealing their inherent qualities and strengths. In Akan culture, names are seen as a vital connection to one's soul purpose, guiding one's journey and helping one fulfil one's true calling. Understanding the vibrations of these names allows individuals to embrace their authentic selves and walk in alignment with their God-given purpose.

CHAPTER 5
The Mystery Of Surnames

A surname is a family name passed down from generation to generation and is typically used to identify individuals belonging to a particular family or lineage. In most cultures, it is added to a person's given name (or first name) to form their full name. Surnames often reflect a family's heritage, occupation, geographical origin, or other ancestral characteristics. For example, in Western cultures, a surname like "Smith" might indicate an ancestor who worked as a metalworker, while "London" might suggest a connection to the city of London. Surnames are commonly inherited from one's parents, often the father, but naming conventions can vary based on cultural or regional practices.

Surnames are not just markers of familial identity but can carry deep spiritual significance that influences one's destiny. Sometimes, a surname can become a curse, an embargo, or a limitation, especially when tied to ancestral practices or past generations' actions. In certain African cultures, such as in Ghana, surnames can reveal the spiritual heritage of a family, and some individuals may unknowingly carry the weight of their forebears' choices and actions. For instance, a person who inherits the surname of an ancestor who was once a fetish priest or priestess may find that they are also bearing the spiritual burden that goes with such a lineage. The ancestral spirits tied to those names can negatively impact a person's life. This idea suggests that surnames carry spiritual significance. For individuals with surnames tied to negative histories, these inherited influences can manifest as setbacks, blockages, or recurring patterns of failure, poverty, or misfortune. The spirits associated with the names of ancestors—particularly those involved in practices such as witchcraft, idolatry, or other forms of spiritual bondage—may continue to exert influence over their descendants until a deliberate and conscious effort is made to break free from their hold. Until such surnames are spiritually dealt with—through prayers, renunciation, or even name changes—the individual may find it difficult to break free from the patterns and limitations set before them by their ancestors. This is why it is crucial not to take surnames for granted. A negative surname can be a subtle force preventing a person from advancing in life, while a surname tied to a righteous or noble lineage may have a positive effect, empowering an individual to achieve their full potential.

In the Bible, we see an example of the power of names and their influence. Jesus Himself changed the names of His disciples to align them with their divine purposes. In Matthew 16:18 (NIV), Jesus says to Simon, **"And I tell you that you are Peter, and on this rock, I will build my church, and the gates of Hades will not overcome it."** By renaming Simon to Peter, which means "rock," Jesus was not merely altering his name but was shifting his identity and destiny, aligning him with the divine purpose of being the foundational leader of the church. In addition to giving Simon the name "Peter," Jesus surnamed several of His disciples, signifying their divine purpose and transforming their identities. One notable example is the renaming of James and John. In Mark 3:16-17 (NIV), it is written: **"These are the twelve He appointed: Simon (to whom He gave the name Peter); James son of Zebedee and his brother John (to them He gave the name Boanerges, which means 'sons of thunder')."**

By giving them the name "Boanerges," meaning "sons of thunder," Jesus signified their fiery passion and boldness in spreading the gospel. This renaming was not just a change of name but a declaration of their future role in God's kingdom. It symbolized their transformation from ordinary fisherfolk to mighty messengers of the Gospel, whose zeal and courage would echo throughout their ministry.

The changing of names, particularly in the case of Peter, James, and John, shows how names are tied to a person's mission and calling. Just as Simon's identity and purpose were realigned with his new name, so too can the proper spiritual intervention—such as renouncing the wrong surname or breaking free from ancestral curses associated with a name—realign a person's destiny and align them with God's intended purpose for their life. This scriptural truth emphasizes the power of names and surnames in shaping one's life and divine destiny.

The Description Of Paul And Barnabas

In the Bible, Barnabas and Paul are associated with Mercury and Jupiter during an event in Lystra, as recorded in Acts 14:8-13. This association is not about astrology but rather about the people in Lystra misunderstanding their roles and mistaking them for the Greek gods Mercury and Jupiter (also known as Hermes and Zeus in Greek mythology). Here is the context and reasoning:

Acts 14:8-13 (NIV):

In Lystra, Paul and Barnabas were preaching the gospel, and Paul healed a man who had been lame from birth. When the people saw the miraculous healing, they mistakenly thought that Paul and Barnabas were gods in human form. They began to call Barnabas

"Jupiter" (the Roman equivalent of Zeus, the king of the gods in Greek mythology) and Paul "Mercury" (the Roman equivalent of Hermes, the messenger of the gods), likely because Paul did most of the speaking. At the same time, Barnabas played a more prominent leadership role. Here's the specific passage:

Acts 14:12-13 (NIV): "Barnabas they called Zeus, and Paul they called Hermes because he was the chief speaker. The priest of Zeus, whose temple was just outside the city, brought bulls and wreaths to the city gates because he and the crowd wanted to offer sacrifices to them."

Why were they given these names?

Barnabas as "Jupiter" (Zeus): Barnabas was the more distinguished or imposing figure between the two, and in the Roman world, Zeus (Jupiter) was considered the king of the gods. The people in Lystra saw Barnabas as a leader, and thus, they assigned him the name of Zeus, the chief god in their pantheon.

Paul as "Mercury" (Hermes): Paul did most of the speaking and was more eloquent, which made people think of him as Hermes, the god of communication, eloquence, and speech. In Roman mythology, Mercury was the messenger of the gods, known for his quickness and eloquence.

This event illustrates the misunderstanding of the people of Lystra, who did not recognize that the apostles were human messengers of the true God. Paul and Barnabas adamantly rejected these titles, promptly correcting the crowd, insisting they were not gods but servants of the living God. While Paul and Barnabas did not accept the names the people of Lystra gave them, claiming they were mere human servants of the true God, there may have been an underlying truth in the people's perception of them. The people, in their limited understanding, associated Paul with Mercury (Hermes) and Barnabas with Jupiter (Zeus) because of the roles they played in the ministry, and this can offer an intriguing reflection of the broader influence that celestial or planetary archetypes can have on people's lives.

Paul's eloquence, quick thinking, and ability to communicate powerfully might have mirrored the characteristics attributed to Mercury, the god of communication, and intellect. Similarly, Barnabas, who often took on a more leadership-driven role characterized by wisdom and authority, may have reflected the qualities associated with Jupiter, the king of gods, known for rulership, guidance, and influence.

While Paul and Barnabas were adamant in rejecting the divine titles, the people's response to them might reveal how human actions, demeanour, and even the impact of spiritual gifts can resonate with archetypal qualities—qualities often attributed to the celestial bodies in various cultural beliefs. In this sense, their lives and behaviours could have embodied aspects of these planetary influences, even if the names themselves were misguided.

This incident reminds us that our lives and actions can sometimes reflect broader cosmic or spiritual patterns, even if we do not consciously embrace them. Though Paul and Barnabas did not accept the titles of gods, how they operated within their divine calling might have mirrored the influence of these planetary bodies in ways that the people of Lystra, unfamiliar with God's true purpose for them, misinterpreted as divine figures. Thus, while their conduct was rooted in God's mission, there could be an element of truth in how their roles and gifts reflected the influence of cosmic archetypes.

Acts 14:14-15 (NIV): "But when the apostles Barnabas and Paul heard of this, they tore their clothes and rushed out into the crowd, shouting, 'Friends, why are you doing this? We, too, are only human, like you. We are bringing you good news, telling you to turn from these worthless things to the living God, who made the heavens and the earth and the sea and everything in them."

Thus, the people of Lystra gave the names Mercury and Jupiter in their misunderstanding. They mistakenly associated Paul and Barnabas with their gods due to their miraculous works. The name change was not a divine or spiritual choice but a cultural response to the apostles' actions that mistakenly led the people to idolize them.

CHAPTER 6
Good And Bad Names

As the introductory paragraph defines, a name is one's identity and reputation. Proverbs 22:1 (NIV) states, *"A good name is more desirable than great riches; to be esteemed is better than silver or gold."* While some may argue that wealth holds more excellent value than a good name, a closer analysis of the scripture reveals otherwise. A good name carries far-reaching influence and is more valuable than riches. It can create opportunities and open doors that wealth alone cannot. Riches may bring material possessions but cannot guarantee the respect and trust that go with a good name.

In society, some affluent individuals grapple with tarnished reputations that hinder their ability to navigate their communities with confidence. Their actions and past behaviours are often under intense scrutiny, leading to questions and doubts about their character. Some have compromised their integrity in the pursuit of riches, sacrificing their good names for fleeting gain. In contrast, a reputable name endures, commanding respect and cultivating trust long after material wealth has diminished.

The writer urges us to prioritize cultivating and protecting a good name over pursuing wealth. A good name enhances personal integrity and creates opportunities for growth and success. Conversely, a bad name can tarnish one's image, block significant opportunities, and destroy meaningful relationships. Just as a good name opens doors, a bad name can close them, creating barriers that are difficult to overcome.

The Mystery Of Names

One of the defining characteristics of a good name is its ability to bring opportunities and favour not only to oneself but to others as well. A good name is more than just a pleasant-sounding designation; it is a legacy of trust and reliability. Consider this question: Can your parents' names, your pastor's name, or any other person's name create good opportunities for you? If not, those names have not yet reached the stature of a "good name."

One of the most important prayers one can offer to God is to ask Him to make your name good—an asset that benefits others and reflects His divine nature. God's name is revered as good because it holds the ultimate power to open doors, bestow favour, and transform lives. In His desire to share in His divine nature, He calls us to uphold the same standard for our names.

Our actions and decisions play a vital role in shaping the quality of our name, which in turn defines our identity and reputation. For instance, a person who frequently indulges in alcohol may come to be known as a drunkard. Likewise, someone engaged in extramarital relationships may be labeled a womanizer, while a lack of restraint with food might result in being called a glutton. These labels, born from behavior, significantly affect how we are perceived both socially and spiritually.

On the other hand, positive deeds and virtuous behavior create good names. Acts of kindness, generosity, and integrity build trust and admiration, fostering a reputation that aligns with honourable qualities. These reputations extend beyond the physical realm and carry weight in the spiritual domain, affecting access to opportunities and relationships.

A good name is a vital asset, opening doors, earning trust, and creating lasting favour. It transcends material wealth, shaping one's legacy and influence in both social and spiritual spheres. By striving to earn a good name, we secure benefits far beyond riches' fleeting rewards.

Examples of Characters with Good and Bad Names

Throughout both Scripture and history, many individuals bear names that reflect their character, actions, and the legacies they left behind. These names often carry deep significance, revealing the virtues or vices they embodied. Let us explore a few examples that illustrate the power of a good name—and the consequences of a bad one.

Characters with Good Names

1. Abraham (Genesis 17:5kjv)

Abraham, initially named Abram, is one of the most well-known figures in the Bible. God changed his name to Abraham, meaning "father of many nations," signifying his purpose and identity shift. Abraham's name represents faith, obedience, and the fulfillment of God's promises. His legacy is one of trust in God's plan, and his name has become synonymous with fatherhood in faith and a model for future generations. His story encourages all believers to trust God even when His promises seem far off.

2. David (1 Samuel 16:12-13kjv)

King David's name became synonymous with leadership, integrity, and heartfelt worship. Though he was not without flaws, David was remembered as a man after God's own heart (Acts 13:22). His name came to represent the ideal of someone who, despite personal shortcomings, earnestly sought to fulfill God's will. His deep devotion to God defined his reign, and the divine promises made to him extended through his lineage.

David's name endured because it reflected a life committed to honoring and glorifying God.

3. Mary, the Mother of Jesus (Luke 1:28kjv)

Mary, the mother of Jesus, is another example of someone with a good name. Her name, "beloved" or "wished for a child," reflects purity, humility, and submission to God's will. Mary is revered not only for her role as the mother of the Savior but also for her faithfulness and obedience. Her name represents faithfulness and courage, as she accepted God's will for her life, even when it brought uncertainty and hardship.

4. Daniel (Daniel 1:6-7kjv)

Daniel's name, "God is my judge," stands for his unwavering commitment to God despite his challenges in a foreign land. As a young man in Babylon, Daniel was determined not to defile himself with the king's food and sought to honor God in all his actions. His name reflected his integrity, wisdom, and deep reliance on God. Daniel's name became synonymous with faithfulness, courage, and divine wisdom.

Characters with Bad Names

1. Jezebel (1 Kings 16:31kjv)

Jezebel is often used as a symbol of wickedness, idolatry, and manipulation. As the queen of Israel, she led the people into the worship of false gods and became infamous for her cruelty, particularly toward the prophets of God. Her name has become synonymous with wickedness, rebellion, and spiritual adultery. While her physical beauty may have earned her favor in the eyes of some, her actions and legacy tarnished her name. Jezebel's example warns about the destructive power of pride and disobedience.

2. Cain (Genesis 4:9-15kjv)

Cain, the firstborn son of Adam and Eve, is remembered for the murder of his brother Abel. His name has become synonymous with jealousy, sin, and rejection of God's favour. Despite God's warning, Cain allowed his anger and pride to dictate his actions, leading to his downfall. His name is often associated with rebellion and violence, and his life serves as a tragic example of how unrepentant sin can ruin one's legacy.

3. Ahab (1 Kings 16:30-33kjv)

King Ahab of Israel is another figure whose name has become associated with wickedness and idolatry. He married Jezebel, and together, they led Israel further into sin, particularly with the worship of Baal. Ahab's reign was marked by his failure to uphold righteousness, and his name has become synonymous with weak leadership and moral corruption. Despite his opportunities for repentance, Ahab's legacy remains tainted by his decisions.

4. Judah (Genesis 38kjv)

Although Judah's name is part of the lineage of Jesus Christ, his personal life had a period where his name was tainted by immorality. In Genesis 38, Judah engaged in actions that brought shame to his family, including the inappropriate treatment of his daughter-in-law, Tamar. While he later repented and played a significant role in preserving his family during a time of famine (Genesis 44:18-34), his earlier actions created a blot on his name. His story illustrates that while redemption is attainable, the consequences of one's actions can leave a lasting stain on a reputation.

The Power of Names

Both good and bad names serve as powerful tools for reflection and understanding. They are not just identifiers but convey deeper truths about the individual's character, actions, and legacy. The Bible gives many examples of how a name can uplift or tarnish a person's legacy. Whether it is a name representing faithfulness and courage, like David, or a name representing wickedness, like Jezebel, the Scriptures show us that the names we carry hold significant weight. The Bible teaches that our names, both given by others and by God, matter. They reflect our lives, our choices, and our destinies. While we cannot always control the names given to us at birth, we can certainly influence the legacy of our name by living lives that honor God. Just as the names of biblical figures have left a long-lasting legacy, our own names can reflect God's grace and goodness. Through righteous actions and strong belief, we become living testimonies of His love and faithfulness.

CHAPTER 7
The Power Of Spiritual Identity

One's identity is not just a name or title; it also signifies one's rank or position, which carries with it authority and responsibility. Just as there are well-established ranks within various societal systems—such as the police service, university staff structure, and corporate organizations—there are also spiritual ranks within the spiritual realm. These ranks determine the extent of an individual's influence, as well as the spirits and forces under their command.

For instance, the Ghana Police Service has a hierarchy of ranks delineating authority and responsibility. At the top, you have the Inspector General of Police (IGP), followed by ranks such as Commissioner of Police, Assistant Commissioner, Chief Superintendent, and down to lower ranks like Constables. Each rank comes with distinct levels of command and responsibility. A Constable has a different level of authority from an IGP, and their access to information, decision-making power, and influence are distinct. In the same way, an individual's position in the spiritual realm determines which spirits, whether good or evil, will be subject to them.

Similarly, within academic institutions, staff members are assigned different ranks based on their experience and ability. In universities, you find positions such as Lecturer, Senior Lecturer, Associate Professor, Professor, and Dean, each with increasing authority and academic standing. A Lecturer has less authority than a professor, who oversees major academic decisions. The higher one's rank, the greater the responsibility and influence over others within that system. Spiritually, the higher an individual's rank, the greater their command over spiritual forces.

In the corporate world, companies often have hierarchical structures where employees are given various ranks, such as Junior Staff, Senior Staff, Managers, Directors, and Executives. Each step up the corporate ladder brings greater decision-making authority, increased influence, and access to highly confidential information. Just as an Executive has far more authority over business decisions than a Junior Staff member, those who ascend in the spiritual realm have greater authority over demonic forces and angelic beings.

In the spiritual realm, there are distinct ranks, much like those in earthly hierarchies. In Ephesians 6:12 (NIV), the Apostle Paul refers to the "***spiritual forces of evil in the heavenly realms***," implying varying levels of spiritual entities. These include high-ranking angels, such as Archangels, with greater authority and power than lower-ranking ones. Similarly, demons also have ranks, from principalities and powers to rulers of darkness. A believer's spiritual rank determines the level of authority they can exercise over spiritual forces. Just as a constable cannot command a commissioner in law enforcement, a new believer does not automatically carry the same level of spiritual authority as a seasoned, mature Christian when confronting principalities and powers.

Just as earthly rank structures define access to authority, spiritual rank dictates an individual's influence in the spiritual realm. The higher one's spiritual position, the greater their ability to command spiritual forces. This emphasizes the importance of nurturing one's spiritual identity, as it directly affects the forces subject to them and the impact they can have in the world.

Understanding your rank in the spiritual realm reveals the extent of your authority and the spirits you can command. Much like in the corporate world, where you cannot exceed your designated level or intrude into a superior's domain, your spiritual rank determines your influence and the spirits under your command. Recognizing your position ensures you operate within rightful boundaries, avoiding overstepping your authority.

However, proponents of the "New Creation" doctrine may not easily accept this truth. They often argue that since all power and authority have been granted to believers, they can command any spirit without regard to spiritual rank. While it is true that believers have access to power, this view overlooks the need to recognize one's spiritual position and the structure of authority in the spiritual realm. Just as one cannot claim authority in an organization without the proper position, one cannot exercise limitless spiritual authority without acknowledging the established spiritual order.

The story of the Sons of Sceva in Acts 19:13-16 (NIV) provides a powerful illustration of how spiritual rank determines the extent of one's authority. In this passage, individuals tried to operate beyond their established spiritual standing, resulting in a humiliating failure. This incident offers profound lessons on spiritual authority and the importance of recognizing one's place within the spiritual hierarchy.

The Mystery Of Names

The scripture reads:

> ***"Some Jews who went around driving out evil spirits tried to invoke the name of the Lord Jesus over those who were demon-possessed. They would say, 'In the name of Jesus, whom Paul preaches, I command you to come out.' Seven sons of Sceva, a Jewish chief priest, were doing this. One day, the evil spirit answered them, 'Jesus I know, and Paul I know about, but who are you?' Then, the man who had the evil spirit jumped on them and overpowered them all. He gave them such a beating that they ran out of the house naked and bleeding."***

Acts 19:13-16 (NIV)

In this dramatic episode, the Sons of Sceva, seven men who were sons of a Jewish chief priest, tried to cast out an evil spirit using the name of Jesus. However, they were not authorised or equipped to operate in the same spiritual capacity as Paul, whose ministry was backed by the power and authority of God. They lacked the requisite spiritual rank and control to confront the demon on those terms. The result was disastrous and a mess: the demon, aware of both Jesus and Paul, rejected the invocation of the name of Jesus by these men, recognizing them as spiritually inferior. The evil spirit then overpowered them, leaving them humiliated, stripped of their clothes, and bleeding. This story offers valuable insight into the principle that spiritual authority is directly tied to one's relationship with God and the divine rank granted by the Holy Spirit. In the spiritual realm, rank is not about position or status, but rather about the legitimacy of one's authority, which is earned through maturity, obedience, and submission to God's will.

The Sons of Sceva attempted to exercise the authority of Jesus without possessing the relationship or spiritual standing to back it up. Their failure illustrates that spiritual authority cannot be borrowed or imitated; it must be personally owned and bestowed by God. Just as in the natural world, where one cannot assume a position of leadership without the necessary credentials, spiritual authority is not simply declared, but earned through alignment with God's divine order.

The response of the evil spirit, "Jesus I know, and Paul I know about, but who are you?" highlights the critical importance of spiritual rank. The demon acknowledged the authority of Jesus and Paul because they were granted spiritual authority by God. However, the Sons of Sceva were unknown in the spiritual realm due to their lack of alignment and divine backing, leaving them vulnerable. This underscores the fact that spiritual authority is not about claiming power, but about being commissioned by God to act in His name. This incident serves as a stark reminder of the significance of understanding and respecting one's spiritual authority. Just as rank determines influence and responsibility in natural systems like corporate or military structures, it applies equally in the spiritual realm. A believer's ability to confront the forces of darkness is directly tied to their spiritual maturity and alignment with God's will. Those who are spiritually immature lack the authority to command the same level of power as those who are well-grounded in their relationship with God.

The Sons of Sceva understood the power of Jesus' name, but they lacked the spiritual authority to wield it effectively. Spiritual authority cannot be manipulated or used without the necessary foundation of a genuine relationship with God. It requires authenticity, a deep understanding of one's spiritual standing, and awareness of the divine order governing the spirit realm.

This story emphasizes that spiritual authority cannot be assumed or borrowed; it must be earned through consistent alignment with God's will. Just as a police officer cannot exceed their rank or a manager cannot issue directives beyond their role, believers are limited by their spiritual position in Christ. Every believer must grow into the authority granted by God, which involves cultivating a strong relationship with Him, walking in His truth, and adhering to His divine purpose.

In conclusion, the failure of the Sons of Sceva offers a crucial lesson on the importance of recognizing and respecting spiritual rank. While anyone can invoke the name of Jesus, wielding His power effectively requires alignment with God's will and the authority that comes from a personal relationship with Him. Just as rank defines one's influence in any structured organization, it is our relationship with God that determines the extent of our spiritual authority and the forces we are empowered to command.

CHAPTER 8
The Power Of The Name Of Jesus

In the Scriptures, a truth reveals the power inherent in the name of Jesus Christ. When Jesus called His disciples, He gave them authority and power to fulfill His work. In Luke 10:1 (NIV), we read, *"After this, the Lord appointed seventy-two others and sent them two by two ahead of him to every town and place where he was about to go."* He equipped them for a specific mission, giving them a mandate that carried His divine authority. But what was the source of this power? It was none other than His name. This truth is further emphasised in Luke 10:17-19 (NIV), where the disciples return to Jesus, filled with excitement and awe. The scripture reads, *"The seventy-two returned with joy and said, 'Lord, even the demons submit to us in your name.' He replied, 'I saw Satan fall like lightning from heaven. I have given you authority to trample on snakes and scorpions and to overcome all the power of the enemy; nothing will harm you."* Notice the emphasis on the name of Jesus. The disciples reported that all the spirits were subject to *His name*, not to their power or authority, but to the divine power and supremacy of Jesus' name.

Why were the spirits subjected to His name? The answer lies in the name of Jesus being above every other name. Philippians 2:9-10 (NIV) declares, *"Therefore God exalted him to the highest place and gave him the name above every name, that at the name of Jesus, every knee should bow, in heaven and on earth and under*

the earth." The name of Jesus is preeminent, supreme, and sovereign, with all authority and dominion resting upon it. It is in His name that we access the power of God, and it is through His name that miracles, deliverances, and healings occur.

We confidently pray in Jesus's name because He holds infinite power and authority. It is not merely a linguistic utterance but a gateway to salvation, deliverance, and miracles. Acts 4:12 (NIV) declares, ***"Salvation is found in no one else, for there is no other name under heaven given to mankind by which we must be saved."*** Jesus' name is the channel through which we receive the grace of salvation, and through His name, we are delivered from the bondage of sin and oppression.

Just as Jesus commissioned His disciples and entrusted them with His name to carry out His mission, we too are empowered by His name to fulfill His purpose in the world. In His name, we confront challenges, overcome spiritual forces, and boldly approach the throne of grace. Every believer who invokes the name of Jesus is aligned with the authority and power resident in Him. This truth is clear in the many instances throughout the Scriptures where the name of Jesus is invoked for healing, deliverance, and breakthrough. The name of Jesus stands as the supreme and all-encompassing power source. We find our identity, authority, and ability to fulfill God's earthly purposes through His name. The name of Jesus is not just a title; it is a divine force that brings salvation, transformation, and victory to all who believe. In His name, we find the fullness of God's grace; through it, we are empowered to live victorious lives.

THE MYSTERY OF THE NAME OF JESUS

Jesus was given different names at various phases or milestones of His life, a truth that is clearly reflected throughout the Holy Scriptures. While we often use terms like 'the Word,' 'Jesus,' 'Jesus Christ,' 'Christ Jesus,' 'Lord,' and 'Christ' interchangeably, it is essential to understand that each name holds a distinct meaning and purpose. These names were conferred upon Him for specific reasons, each corresponding to a different aspect of His divine identity and mission.

To illustrate, consider an ordinary person named Nathan. When addressing him, you would use his name, Nathan. However, if Nathan earns a title, such as 'Prophet,' it is necessary to refer to him by that title, as it now forms part of his identity. In this context, Nathan would no longer be 'Nathan'; he would be known as 'Prophet Nathan,' and the title reflects his new role and authority. Similarly, while the various names of Jesus all refer to the same person, they highlight different dimensions of His purpose and mission.

At the beginning of His life, He was not known by the name 'Jesus'; He was referred to as 'the Word' (John 1:1). This designation was significant and foundational in understanding His role in creation and His relationship with God the Father. As we progress through Scripture, we see how His identity evolved, each marking a new phase in His divine journey—culminating in the name 'Jesus,' which embodies His earthly mission of salvation. Each name that Jesus bears, though referring to the same person, emphasizes a different part of His divinity, humanity, and purpose. Understanding these distinctions allows us to fully appreciate the depth of His mission and the eternal significance of His name.

This is confirmed in the opening verse of the Gospel of John, which says:

> ***"In the beginning was the Word, and the Word was with God, and the Word was God." – John 1:1 (KJV)***

This scripture highlights that before Jesus became manifest in the flesh, He existed as the Word. Acknowledging Christ as the Word is foundational to the Christian faith, as it reveals His divine nature and eternal existence before His incarnation. This understanding deepens our grasp of the pre-incarnate Christ and His place in the heavenly realm. A powerful affirmation of this truth is found in 1 John 5:7, which declares:

> ***"For there are three that bear record in heaven, the Father, the Word, and the Holy Ghost: and these three are one." – 1 John 5:7 (KJV)***

This verse speaks to the unity of the Father, the Word, and the Holy Ghost, reaffirming that the Word was indeed a part of the eternal Godhead before Jesus was manifest on earth. This may challenge some conventional thinking, but it underscores the reality that the Word, before assuming the name Jesus, was known by the entire universe and even the multiversal realm of God. The name "Jesus" was given to Him specifically for His earthly mission: to save humanity from sin. As the angel declared to Mary, ***"You shall call His name Jesus, for He will save His people from their sins"*** (Matthew 1:21). The name "Jesus" was thus linked to His purpose and assignment on earth: salvation.

It is essential to understand that the Word and Jesus refer to the same divine person, but they highlight various aspects of His identity. The Word represents His eternal, divine nature, while Jesus reflects His incarnate, earthly role as the Savior of humanity. Although these names are distinct, they both point to the same person—the second person of the Holy Trinity—who came to fulfill the will of God through His earthly ministry.

Just as there is a distinction between *The Word* and *Jesus*, there is also a distinction between *Jesus* and *Christ*. *Jesus* refers to the Son of Man, the earthly manifestation of God who lived among humans, walked, and experienced the trials and challenges of life. On the other hand, *Christ* refers to the Son of God, the anointed one.

Jesus is the Savior of men, who came to earth to redeem humanity from sin. He is the one who lived a sinless life, died on the cross, and resurrected on the third day to offer eternal life to those who believe in Him. Christ embodies the anointing, divine power, and the very presence of God that make salvation possible. The title "Christ" refers to the Messiah, God's chosen one, upon whom the Spirit rests and through whom humanity receives redemption. While "Jesus" is the personal name of the Savior, "Christ" encapsulates the divine purpose and anointing that enables God's plan of salvation to unfold for all people. Thus, Jesus and Christ are distinct yet interconnected—Jesus, the man who walked the earth, embodying love, and sacrifice; Christ, the divine authority and anointing that empowered His mission, transcending time, and space. Together, they form the bridge between humanity and divinity, revealing the boundless glory of God.

After His crucifixion, death, and resurrection, God conferred a new name upon Jesus. This name was not just a title but a new rank, authority, and office in the spirit realm. It was the name "Lord" and "Christ."This can be seen in Acts 2:36 (KJV), where it is written:

"Therefore, let all Israel be assured of this: God has made this Jesus, whom you crucified, both Lord and Christ."

The titles "Lord" and "Christ" signify Jesus's exalted position in the heavens, on earth, and beneath the earth. It is a name above every other name. Philippians 2:11 (NIV) further affirms this: ***"And every tongue acknowledges that Jesus Christ is Lord, to the glory of God the Father."*** The recognition of Jesus as Lord is not limited to humans; every being, whether in the heavens, on earth, or in the underworld, acknowledges His supreme authority.

So, how did Jesus earn the name "Lord"? The Word of God explains that Jesus earned this title through His obedience. Philippians 2:8-9 (NIV) tells us, ***"And being found in appearance as a man, he humbled himself by becoming obedient to death—even death on a cross! Therefore, God exalted him to the highest place and gave him the name above every name."*** Jesus' obedience, even to death on the cross, qualified Him to receive this exalted name. It was through His perfect submission to God's will, even in the most excruciating of circumstances, that He earned the title of "Lord."

God had ordained various names for the Word (Jesus), but these names were not bestowed arbitrarily—they were earned through perfect obedience. It is crucial to understand that Jesus did not simply receive the title of "Lord" by default; He had to walk the path of obedience to earn it. His unwavering willingness to submit to the Father's will, even in the face of unimaginable suffering, elevated Him to His rightful position as Lord of all creation. Today, in the heavenly realm, Jesus is no longer known as Jesus, but as "Lord"—the name above every other name. His perfect obedience to God has positioned Him as the supreme authority in both the spiritual and physical realms. He is exalted above all, and His name commands universal reverence.

The book of Revelation also tells us that God has prepared a new name for each believer. Revelation 2:17 (NIV) says: "Whoever has ears, let them hear what the Spirit says to the churches. To the victorious one, I will give some of the hidden manna. I will also give that person a white stone with a new name written on it, known only to the one who receives it." This new name reflects your spiritual identity and is only earned through faithful obedience to His will. Just as Jesus' obedience led to His exaltation, our obedience will unlock the destiny God has in store for us and the new name He has prepared for us as our eternal reward.

CHAPTER 9
Inheritances In Christ

In His infinite grace, God has prepared several inheritances for the saints in Christ. These include the inheritance of the Kingdom, blessings, all things, and, most notably, the inheritance of a name. However, God will not entrust these inheritances to us until we are fully matured and prepared to steward them faithfully. As the Apostle Paul declared, "***Now I commit you to God and to the word of his grace, which can build you up and give you an inheritance among all who are sanctified***" (Acts 20:32, NIV). For the purpose of this discourse, we will focus on one specific inheritance: the inheritance of a name.

The Scriptures reveal that Christ inherited a name far superior to any other. The writer of Hebrews states, "***So he became as much superior to the angels as the name he has inherited is superior to theirs***" (Hebrews 1:4, NIV). This name signifies Christ's authority, position, and identity as the Son of God, exalted above all creation.

The Significance of the Inheritance of a Name

In biblical times, a name carried immense significance, representing one's identity, authority, and destiny. Names were more than mere labels; they reflected a person's divine purpose and calling. When Christ inherited a more excellent name, it signified His unique position as the exalted Savior and Lord, far above every principality, power, and authority. His name is not merely a title; it reflects His divine mission and the ultimate victory over sin and death. It is the seal of His redemptive work and divine supremacy.

However, this inheritance of a name is not exclusive to Christ alone. As heirs of God and joint heirs with Christ (Romans 8:17), believers are called to share in the inheritance of His name. Through our union with Christ, we are invited to partake in the authority, privileges, and blessings His name embodies. Through Him, we gain access to the heavenly riches of this inheritance, which includes the power to stand before God with confidence and claim His promises.

Yet, this inheritance is not granted indiscriminately. In His wisdom, God requires that we undergo a process of spiritual growth and preparation before we are entrusted with such a vast inheritance. As Acts 20:32 emphasizes, the Word of God's grace sanctifies, strengthens, and builds us up to bear the weight of this glorious inheritance. God's plan is not for us to receive a name casually, but to be shaped by His grace into vessels worthy of the honor and responsibility that come with it. One of the rewards God has prepared for His people is the inheritance of a name. Just as Christ inherited a more excellent name, believers are called to share in the authority and glory that His name carries. However, this inheritance is not passive; it requires a journey of spiritual growth, sanctification, and transformation. Only through God's grace can we be equipped to steward the name and authority entrusted to us, reflecting His glory in every aspect of our lives.

The Purpose of Christ's Coming: The Inheritance of a Name

The primary purpose of Christ's coming into the world was to obtain a name—an inheritance reserved for Him by God. His death, crucifixion, and resurrection were necessary steps to achieve that goal. Christ had to endure obedience and sacrifice to receive the reward God had prepared for Him. Through His victory, He earned the exalted title of "Lord," a name that commands reverence in heaven, on earth, and beneath the earth. Through His obedience, even unto death, He was granted the name above all names, signifying His eternal authority and dominion.

The Name God Has Prepared for You

Have you ever wondered why God created you and assigned you a specific purpose? Just as Christ came into the world to obtain a name, your life on earth is tied to the same divine objective. You were created to earn a name—an identity of eternal significance in heaven, on earth, and beneath the earth. The name God desires to give you is not just a title; it reflects your spiritual authority, your place in His eternal kingdom, and your unique role in His divine plan. The Scriptures speak of this hidden name, known only to God: "To the one who is victorious… I will also give that person a white stone with a new name written on it, known only to the one who receives it" (Revelation 2:17, NIV). This name is reserved for those who endure, remain faithful to their divine calling, and overcome life's challenges with obedience.

Just as Christ fulfilled His purpose to obtain His name, your mission on earth is to earn a name that carries eternal significance. This name represents your rank, authority, and legacy within God's kingdom. It transcends the earthly realm, and bears witness both in the spiritual and worldly domains. If you do not obtain this name, no matter your earthly achievements, you will have missed the ultimate purpose for which you were created.

Pursuing the Heavenly Name

The pursuit of this heavenly name should be your highest priority. It demands steadfast obedience, faithfulness, and a commitment to fulfilling God's purpose for your life. Like Christ, you are expected to walk the path set before you, knowing that this journey will lead you to the glorious inheritance God has prepared for you. This inheritance is not merely a reward but a reflection of your transformation and alignment with God's divine will. The inheritance of a name in Christ is not just about receiving a title; it is about stepping into a divine identity, authority, and purpose with eternal ramifications. As you grow spiritually, embrace God's grace, and walk in obedience, you will receive the name God has prepared for you, which will testify to your faithfulness and position in His eternal kingdom.

CHAPTER 10
Naming Ceremony

The conduct of naming ceremonies varies significantly from one culture to another, and while the Bible does not prescribe a specific format, dedicating a child to the Lord is scriptural. This dedication process, often symbolized by christening or a similar ceremony, reflects a biblical tradition of consecrating children and acknowledging God's sovereignty over their lives.

The birth of Jesus marked a pivotal moment in history, fulfilling numerous prophecies, including those related to the dedication of God's children. Born during the Feast of Tabernacles, a time rich with spiritual significance, Jesus was presented in the Temple on the eighth day of His life. This act fulfilled the prophecy spoken by the prophet Haggai in Haggai 2:9, which declares, "The glory of this latter house shall be greater than of the former, saith the Lord of hosts: and in this place will I give peace, saith the Lord of hosts." While this prophecy primarily referred to the physical temple, it also pointed to its ultimate fulfillment in Christ, who would bring peace and salvation to the world. Jesus' dedication on the eighth day was both a symbolic and prophetic act, showing that even the Son of God respected the customs of His time, while simultaneously fulfilling God's divine plan for salvation.

Similarly, the early Church also experienced a form of "dedication." The Church was born during the Feast of First fruits, and the Holy Spirit came upon the disciples on Pentecost, a celebration rich in prophetic and spiritual significance. This marks the moment when the Church was "dedicated" to its mission on earth, empowered by the Holy Spirit to continue the work that Christ began. The first fruit offering, symbolizing the beginning of the harvest, parallels the birth of the Church and its dedication to the gospel and God's kingdom work.

The timing and manner in which a child is named and dedicated are of great significance. When a child is born, and parents do not dedicate the child on time or give them the correct name, they risk hindering the child's destiny. Naming and dedicating a child is not merely a cultural practice; it is a spiritual act with profound implications. The Bible emphasizes that names define a person's identity and purpose. As parents or guardians, we have a responsibility to honor God's will by ensuring that the child's spiritual journey begins on the right path. Failure to dedicate a child properly or neglecting to give them a meaningful name can frustrate their destiny and confuse their journey through life. A child who is not committed to God may lack a sense of divine purpose, and without the correct name, they may grow up without a clear understanding of their calling. This neglect can result in an unfulfilled life, as the child will lack the spiritual foundation to navigate life's challenges.

Just as Jesus was dedicated in the Temple on the eighth day and the Church was outdoored at Pentecost, parents have a responsibility to dedicate their children to God and give them names that reflect divine purpose. By doing so, they ensure that the child's life is aligned with God's will, helping them walk in the fullness of their potential. It is essential to approach these acts with reverence and understanding, as the consequences of negligence can be far-reaching, affecting the child's spiritual journey and the fulfillment of their destiny.

While naming ceremonies and christenings may differ across cultures, the biblical precedent for dedicating a child to God and giving them a meaningful name is clear. It is not merely a custom but a spiritual obligation that has lasting effects on the child's identity and purpose. Therefore, parents should be diligent and intentional in dedicating their children to God and choosing names that will empower them to fulfill their God-given purpose on earth.

Who is responsible for Naming a Child?

In various cultures and traditions, naming a child is often viewed as a shared duty between the father and mother. However, when examined through the lens of scripture, the question of who is primarily responsible for naming a child takes on a deeper and more nuanced understanding. The Bible provides clear examples and divine instructions on naming children, revealing that this practice, while necessary for identity and destiny, is rooted in God's sovereignty and the roles assigned to each parent.

The Father's Role in Naming

The father is often depicted throughout the Bible as the primary figure responsible for naming children. The naming of a child is not just a cultural norm but a responsibility that carries profound significance, as it marks the child's identity, destiny, and relationship with God. A powerful example is **Genesis 4:1 (NIV)**: "Adam made love to his wife Eve, and she became pregnant and gave birth to Cain. She said, 'With the help of the Lord, I have brought forth a man.'" Although Eve was the one who gave birth to Cain, it is Adam, the father, who was given the responsibility of naming him, as seen in **Genesis 5:3 (NIV)**: "When Adam had lived 130 years, he had a son in his likeness, in his image; and he named him Seth."

Another important example is the naming of Jesus. The Bible records explicitly in **Matthew 1:21 (NIV)** that the angel instructed Joseph, the earthly father of Jesus, to name the child: "She will give birth to a son, and you are to give him the name Jesus because he will save his people from their sins." Here, God entrusted Joseph, as the father figure, with the significant responsibility of naming the child, thus emphasizing the father's key role in the naming process.

The Role of the Mother

While the father is typically responsible for naming the child, the mother's role is still significant and influential. In **Luke 1:59-60 (NIV)**, we see an example of the mother's involvement in naming the child, as the Holy Spirit prompted the parents of John the Baptist. "On the eighth day, they came to circumcise the child, and they were going to name him after his father, Zechariah. But his mother spoke up and said, 'No! He is to be called John." This passage shows that, although the father had the legal right to name the child, the mother exercised her authority in declaring the child's name based on God's instruction. In this case, Elizabeth's decision aligned with the divine purpose, proving that the mother can play an active role in shaping the name, especially when it aligns with the Lord's plan.

God's Sovereign Role in Naming

It is important to note that while the father and mother play crucial roles in naming their children, God Himself ultimately holds the authority over the child's identity and name.In **Isaiah 45:5 (NIV)**, God says, "I am the Lord, and there is no other; apart from me, there is no God. I will strengthen you though you have not acknowledged me." God ordains every life's destiny and significance, including the name by which that person will be known.

This truth is also affirmed in the naming of several biblical figures. For instance, in **Genesis 17:5 (NIV)**, God tells Abraham, "No longer will you be called Abram; your name will be Abraham, for I have made you a father of many nations." Similarly, **Genesis 32:28 (NIV)** records God's change of Jacob's name to Israel: "Then the man said, 'Your name will no longer be Jacob, but Israel because you have struggled with God and with humans and have overcome.'" Both examples illustrate how God has the power to change a person's name to reflect their divine calling and purpose.

The Balance Between Parental and Divine Authority

When naming a child, these examples show a balance between parental responsibility and divine authority. While the father is typically responsible for naming, both parents ensure that the name is chosen according to God's will. Moreover, God's sovereign influence should guide the naming process, as He determines the child's purpose and identity.

CHAPTER 11
The Use Of Spiritual Tokens In Christening Ceremonies

Within the body of Christ, certain sects believe that administering tokens during practices such as christening is unnecessary. These individuals contend that Christ is entirely sufficient, and that there is no need for additional symbols or objects in a believer's life. They believe that Christ alone provides everything necessary for spiritual growth and protection.However,this perspective overlooks the significance of tokens in the Scriptures, which serve as meaningful elements of spiritual practice, symbolizing deeper truths and fulfilling specific purposes.The administration of tokens during christening is not only scripturally supported but also essential in easing a child's journey on earth and unveiling them to the new world. Just as we administer tokens over a deceased person's body to honor and protect their passage, it is equally vital to distribute tokens to a newborn. These tokens serve as markers that prepare the child for their earthly journey, imparting spiritual blessings and aligning them with God's purposes.

Standard tokens administered during christening include salt, water, honey, and oil. Each token carries significance and must be applied thoughtfully.

Salt is one of the most ancient and significant tokens in the Bible. In Colossians 4:6, the Apostle Paul instructs believers: "*Let your conversation be always full of grace, seasoned with salt, so you may know how to answer everyone.*"

Salt is applied during christening to set the child's life on fire, stirring their potential and potentizing their tongue. It also forms a protective aura around the child, safeguarding them from evil and harm. Salt symbolizes covenant and preservation, ensuring the child will not escape their divine calling and purpose.

Water, another significant token worth mentioning, is referenced in various biblical texts as a symbol of spiritual cleansing and fruitfulness. In John 7:38 (NIV), Jesus says, "Whoever believes in me, as Scripture has said, rivers of living water will flow from within them." Water is applied to the child during the christening to make them fruitful on earth. It signifies the washing away of sin and the invitation to a life of spiritual vitality and growth. Water symbolizes the believer's rebirth in Christ, offering a fresh start as they enter the world, ready to bear good fruit.

Honey has historically been regarded as a symbol of abundance, sweetness, and promising opportunities. In Proverbs 24:13-14 (NIV), the wisdom of honey is extolled:"***Eat honey, my son, for it is good; honey from the comb is sweet to your taste. Know also that wisdom is like honey for you; if you find it, there is a future hope for you, and your hope will not be cut off.***" Applying honey during christening is a prophetic act, opening the child's eyes to opportunities for prosperity, joy, and success. It ensures that their life will be characterized by sweetness, enhancing their ability to recognize and walk in the good opportunities set before them on the earth.

Oil, often associated with anointing in the Bible, plays a pivotal role in the christening. In Psalm 23:5 (NIV), the psalmist says, "You anoint my head with oil; my cup overflows." Oil is symbolic of the Holy Spirit's presence and empowerment, applied to the child during christening as a sign of anointing for assignment and illumination. It signifies that the child is set apart for God's divine purpose and will be guided by the light of His Spirit as they navigate life's path. Oil imparts wisdom, direction, and divine empowerment for the calling that God has placed on their life.

These tokens—salt, water, honey, and oil—are not merely physical elements but carry deep spiritual significance. They serve as divine markers that empower the child for their journey, offering protection, fruitfulness, opportunities, and the illumination necessary for fulfilling their purpose. They are not magical objects; instead, they are physical representations of spiritual truths and blessings that, when applied in faith, activate God's promises in the child's life.

It is crucial to understand that administering these tokens should not be approached lightly or mechanically. Just as applying these elements to a child's life is meant to usher them into the world, it is equally essential that the spiritual meaning and intention behind these actions are clear. The Bible shows us that tokens are anointed with purpose and must be applied accordingly. As seen in various biblical practices and through the example of Christ's dedication, the application of tokens during christening is not merely a ritual but a powerful act of spiritual impartation. By applying these tokens, parents, spiritual leaders, and guardians align the child's life with God's will, ensuring they are well-equipped to walk in their divine purpose. Salt, water, honey, and oil represent potent aspects of God's divine provision for the child's life. As such, these tokens must be administered with care and understanding, as they serve as crucial elements in preparing the child for a life of purpose, blessing, and spiritual fulfillment.

CHAPTER 12
The Names Of The Blood

The name we assign to something influences its role or function. Unfortunately, we often give names without fully considering their intended purpose, which can result in the thing not fulfilling its potential. In the Bible, there are many concepts that we tend to use interchangeably, believing they are the same, yet their roles are distinct. A prime example of this is the way we have sometimes handled the different names associated with the blood. In this chapter, we will explore the significance of the names of the blood, specifically the blood of the Lamb, and the distinct role each type of blood plays in our lives. Just as there are various blood groups and classifications, there are also various kinds of blood in the spiritual context, each with its unique function. There are three categories of the blood of the Lamb: the blood of Jesus, the blood of Jesus Christ, and the blood of Christ. While they may seem similar, they are not the same, and it is crucial to understand the distinct roles of each so that they are not misappropriated or misapplied. The following pages will explore these aspects to understand their implications and power better.

The Blood Of Jesus

Hebrews 10:19 (KJV) says:

"Having therefore, brethren, boldness to enter into the holiest by the blood of Jesus.

The blood of Jesus is meant explicitly for sinners—the lost, those who are still in their sinful nature and have not yet received the transforming life of God. It is essential to understand that as a believer, you are no longer identified as a sinner. The moment you confessed Jesus as your Lord, you were transferred from the domain of darkness into the marvelous light of God's kingdom. You were born of God, and the divine seed of Christ now dwells in you. If you are still struggling with the idea of being a sinner, it reflects a lack of clarity regarding the foundational truths of your faith. You must recognize that the moment you accepted Jesus Christ, you were sealed with His righteousness and no longer carry the old sinful nature. It is vital not to confuse acts of sin with the nature of sin. While acts of sin are indeed wrong, they do not define you as a sinner if the seed of God—Christ—abides in you. The key distinction is this: as a believer, you are declared righteous through the blood of Jesus and are no longer bound by the sinful nature. The blood of Jesus serves a specific purpose for those who are situated in the outer courts of salvation—the unsaved, those still outside the covenant family of God. In His infinite wisdom, God instructed Solomon to construct a temple that embodied His divine plan for communion with humanity. The temple was divided into three distinct courts: the outer court, the middle court, and the innermost court. Each court stood for a progressive level of access to the presence of God, with each stage requiring specific offerings and sacrifices for entry.

The outer court was a space where individuals from various backgrounds and spiritual conditions congregated. It was open to all who sought to approach the presence of God, regardless of their spiritual standing or heritage. Among those gathered in the outer court were the Gentiles, seekers of truth who were not part of the covenant people of Israel but were drawn by a desire to know the God of Abraham, Isaac, and Jacob. The temple was divided into three distinct courts: the outer court, the middle court, and the innermost court. Each court symbolized a progressive level of access to the presence of God, with each stage requiring specific offerings and sacrifices for entry. Within these courts were also the unclean—those restricted from entering the inner sanctuaries due to ceremonial or moral impurity. New converts and penitents seeking to reconcile with God and build a relationship with Him also found their place in the outer court.

The outer court was characterized by its accessibility, where the first steps toward redemption could be taken. While it allowed proximity to the temple, it did not grant access to the more intimate courts, where deeper fellowship with God was experienced. The blood of Jesus, therefore, is indispensable for those who find themselves in the "outer court" of their spiritual journey. It serves as the cleansing agent that removes the barrier of sin, enabling them to move from a distant approach to a closer communion with the Father.

Through the blood of Jesus, those who once stood on the fringes of God's presence are granted access to His kingdom. They are empowered to transition from the outer court, the realm of initial contact and repentance, into the middle and innermost courts, where the fullness of divine fellowship and spiritual intimacy unfolds. This progression is the transformative journey from estrangement to reconciliation, from being strangers to becoming sons and daughters of God. Thus, the blood of Jesus serves as the gateway for sinners—the redemptive force that grants access to God's presence. Once washed in the blood, they are no longer bound by their sinful nature. They are brought into the fold of God's family, able to advance into the middle and innermost courts of His divine presence, where deeper relationships, understanding, and fellowship with the Father are experienced

The Blood Of Jesus Christ

The second kind of blood to consider is the blood of Jesus Christ, which holds a distinct and elevated role compared to the blood of Jesus. This blood is associated with the middle court of the temple, a sacred space that symbolizes deeper fellowship and spiritual interaction with God. Within this middle court were several significant items, including the menorah (seven-branched candlestick), the table of showbread, and the altar of incense. This court is the spiritual location of the ecclesia (the church), where believers gather as the body of Christ to experience communion with one another and God.

In the church, fellowship among believers plays a pivotal role in spiritual cleansing and sanctification. The Word of God declares, ***"But if we walk in the light, as he is in the light, we have fellowship one with another, and the blood of Jesus Christ his Son cleanseth us from all sin"*** (1 John 1:7, KJV). This scripture emphasizes the power of the blood of Jesus Christ in the context of fellowship. Through this shared communion—both with God and among ourselves—believers experience the ongoing cleansing of sin.

One of the items in the middle court held profound significance. It comprised seven branches, each symbolizing one of the seven churches referenced in the Book of Revelation. These seven churches represent the fullness of the body of Christ, each with its distinct characteristics, challenges, and mission. The continual light of the menorah symbolized the ever-present guidance and illumination provided by the Holy Spirit to the church.

Another key item in the middle court was the table of showbread, which held twelve loaves of bread, symbolizing God's provision, and covenant relationship with His people. Meanwhile, the altar of incense stood for the prayers of the saints ascending to God with a sweet aroma. Together, these elements demonstrated the rich fellowship and active participation in the divine life believers are called to experience in the middle court of worship. Thus, the blood of Jesus Christ is the antidote for believers' sins, cleansing us and enabling us to remain in unbroken fellowship with God and one another. Unlike the blood of Jesus, which brings the unsaved into the kingdom, Jesus Christ sustains those already within the ecclesia, ensuring their sanctification and unity within the body of Christ. This dynamic process reflects God's redemptive power, preparing believers for deeper intimacy with Him in the innermost court. In this light, the blood of Jesus Christ is a means of forgiveness and a continuous agent of cleansing, keeping believers aligned with God's divine purpose and in harmony with the fellowship of the saints.

Do We Ask For Forgiveness from God As Believers?

As believers, we are not called to ask for forgiveness repeatedly but rather to receive the forgiveness already in motion through the finished work of Christ. Forgiveness is not something we must strive to obtain; it has already been procured for us through the sacrifice of Jesus on the cross. It is an established reality that God's grace extended to us freely. The Word of God in Acts 26:18 (KJV) reveals this truth:

> ***"To open their eyes, and to turn them from darkness to light, and from the power of Satan unto God, that they may receive forgiveness of sins, and inheritance among them which are sanctified by faith in me."***

This scripture explicitly states that forgiveness is something to be received, not something we continuously beg for. God has already placed forgiveness in motion by His grace, making it perpetually available to all who believe in Christ. It is a divine provision secured through His blood, ensuring our sins are forgiven and thoroughly washed away.

To receive forgiveness is to acknowledge and embrace what Christ has done on our behalf. It is not about pleading or negotiating with God but about stepping into the reality of what has already been done. As believers, we live under the umbrella of grace, where forgiveness is a constant and active force that reconciles us to God and keeps us in the right standing. When we sin, we are not called to strive for forgiveness as if it were withheld; instead, we confess our sins, trusting in His faithfulness and justice to cleanse us (1 John 1:9). This process is about restoring fellowship, not obtaining forgiveness anew. Thus, forgiveness is not a transaction to be initiated; it is a gift to be received, already made available to us by Jesus's sacrificial love. This understanding frees us from the weight of guilt and empowers us to walk confidently in the light of His grace and truth.

The Blood Of Christ

The **blood of Christ** is a profound and powerful entity, distinct in its function and application from both the **blood of Jesus** and the **blood of Jesus Christ**. In **1 Corinthians 10:16 (KJV)**, the Apostle Paul writes, *"The cup of blessing which we bless, is it not the communion of the blood of Christ?"* This verse highlights the intimate relationship believers share with Christ through His blood, underscoring the sacrificial nature of His offering and the unique place His blood holds in our redemption. The blood of Christ, as we understand it, corresponds to the innermost court of the Tabernacle, the **Most Holy Place**, where God's presence dwells in its most whole measure.

The Most Holy Place, within the context of the Tabernacle in the Old Testament, was the holiest part of the sanctuary, separated by a veil, and it was where God's glory manifested in its purest form. Only the high priest could enter this sacred space, and even then, only once a year on the Day of Atonement, bringing the blood of an unblemished sacrifice to offer on behalf of the people. This blood symbolized the cleansing and reconciliation of the people with God. The Most Holy Place represents the ultimate intimacy between God and man, where full communion can be realised.

Now, the **blood of Christ** corresponds to this innermost court, for it is through His blood that we, as believers, are granted access to this place of fellowship with God. Unlike the blood of Jesus, which served as the means of salvation and the initiation into the Kingdom of God, the blood of Christ is what allows us to enter into the presence of God, moving past the outer and middle courts of the Tabernacle to commune directly with God in the Most Holy Place. This is where we find ultimate reconciliation, where the veil is torn, and access to God's presence is freely available to all in Christ.

The blood of Jesus served as the first step in this journey; it is the blood that saved us from our sins, delivered us from the dominion of darkness, and brought us into the light of God's kingdom. It is foundational, but the blood of Christ enables us to dwell in the most profound communion with God in the presence of His holiness. This is a critical distinction, for though they are part of the same redemptive work, their applications differ.

The blood of Jesus Christ is Christ's sacrificial and redemptive work, but the blood of Christ speaks specifically to the ongoing, eternal work of intercession and communion. Through His blood, the believer gains access to the Most Holy Place. It is through the blood of Christ that we are continually sanctified and made holy, enabling us to stand before a holy God without fear. Just as the high priest could not enter the Most Holy Place without the blood of the sacrifice, so too can we not enter the fullness of God's presence without the blood of Christ.

In the New Testament, the blood of Christ grants believers' direct access to God's throne of grace. Through this blood, we can draw near to God confidently and ensure that we are welcomed in, not as strangers, but as sons and daughters. The blood of Christ, unlike the blood of Jesus or the blood of Jesus Christ, is the ultimate sacrifice that opened the way for us to dwell with God in intimate fellowship, unshackled by the restrictions of the old covenant. It is the gateway to the Most Holy Place, where we experience God's presence in its whole and intimate form. The blood of Christ is central to our faith, for through it, we are made holy, sanctified, and brought near to God. It grants us the privilege of entering the Most Holy Place, where His glory resides. This is not a mere formality, but a profound reality that speaks to the restoration of our relationship with God, made possible by Christ's sacrifice. Through His blood, we are invited to live in the fullness of God's presence daily, continually purified, sanctified, and transformed into the image of Christ Himself.

The Holy Communion

When you visit a church or attend a regular service and are presented with Holy Communion, do you perceive the wine as the blood of Christ or Jesus, and do you view the bread as the body of Christ or the body of Jesus? How you interpret these elements is crucial, as it directly affects the spiritual impact they will have on you. The Scriptures warn us of the dangers of failing to properly discern the significance of the body and blood during communion. 1 Corinthians 11:29 says, "For he that eateth and drinketh unworthily, eateth and drinketh damnation to himself, not discerning the Lord's body." As Paul emphasizes, the failure to understand and honor the true nature of these sacred elements can lead to negative consequences, including physical sickness or even death. It is crucial to understand that the bread and wine served during Holy Communion are rightly referred to as the body of Christ and the blood of Christ, not the body of Jesus and the blood of Jesus. When a pastor or minister lifts the elements and refers to them as the body and blood of Jesus, this is a misrepresentation. The correct designation, as stipulated in Scripture, is the body of Christ and the blood of Christ.

This distinction is important because Holy Communion is the glorified, resurrected Christ, not His physical, earthly body that suffered on the cross.Therefore, when partaking in the Eucharist, believers must recognize the sacred reality of what they receive—the life-giving body and blood of Christ, the exalted Lord—rather than mistakenly identifying it with the historical, physical body of Jesus before His resurrection.

Thus, during Communion, the elements should always be properly acknowledged as the body of Christ and the blood of Christ, ensuring both reverence and theological accuracy in worship.Every sacred act, such as the taking of Holy Communion, is bound by higher levels of spiritual understanding, and how we interpret them will directly influence their impact on our lives. If we approach these elements with clarity and reverence, understanding them according to Scripture, it will have a positive, life-giving effect on us. On the other hand, neglecting to recognize their true meaning can hinder the blessings and power they are meant to impart. We must align our practices with the truth of God's Word to ensure that we live in His grace and purpose. Let us not simply follow tradition or rely on popular opinion, but actively seek the truth, speaking and acting according to the knowledge and understanding revealed in Scripture.

Does It Matter How We Name The Holy Communion?

It does. Every meal we partake in carries a deeper spiritual significance, pointing to a greater reality beyond the physical. For example, if someone serves you jollof rice in a dream or vision, you may initially perceive it as just a meal, but in the spiritual realm, it could be the impartation of a spiritual gift. Similarly, ordinary water in a vision might symbolize a viral disease. The physical elements of the meal are often mere symbols of a higher spiritual truth. In the same way, when we refer to Holy Communion as the body and blood of Christ, we acknowledge that these elements are the very source of life. As Scripture says, "Whoso eateth my flesh, and drinketh my blood, hath eternal life; and I will raise him at the last day" (John 6:54, KJV). By partaking in this sacred meal, we are engaging in the life of Christ, drawing that life into our own. It is not just a symbolic act but a profound spiritual reality that has the power to infuse us with Christ's life-giving energy.

Therefore, how we name and understand Holy Communion directly influences its spiritual impact on our lives. By discerning its deeper meaning and calling it by its rightful names—the body and blood of Christ—we align ourselves with the truth of Scripture and allow that truth to work in us, bringing forth life and transformation.

CHAPTER 13
In Whose Name Should Believers Pray?

Prayer, at its core, is a means of participating in God's divine counsel. It is an act of faith that acknowledges God's sovereignty, seeks His intervention, and aligns our hearts with His will. For believers today, the Word of God unequivocally instructs us to pray in the name of Jesus Christ. Jesus Himself said, "And whatsoever ye shall ask in my name, that will I do, that the Father may be glorified in the Son. If ye shall ask anything in my name, I will do it" (John 14:13–14 KJV). This clear command forms the cornerstone of Christian prayer. Before delving into the significance of praying in Jesus' name, it is essential to first explore how prayer was conducted prior to Christ's earthly ministry and the covenantal framework that underpinned those prayers.

Before the advent of Christ, prayer was not offered in His name, as his earthly ministry and atoning work had not yet been fulfilled. Instead, people prayed according to the covenants made between God and their ancestors. These covenants served as both the legal and spiritual frameworks through which humanity could access God. For example, God chose the patriarch Abraham to establish a covenant that would bless all nations. Through this covenant, Abraham and his descendants were granted the privilege of calling upon the name of the Lord. Genesis records, "And he built an altar there, and called upon the name of the Lord" (Genesis 12:8, KJV).

Abraham's descendants—Isaac, Jacob, and the nation of Israel—continued to approach God based on this Abrahamic covenant.

Similarly, prayer in the Old Testament was often directed to God as the covenant-keeping Yahweh (Jehovah) under the Mosaic covenant. Moses interceded on behalf of Israel by appealing to God's promises to their forefathers. When the Israelites sinned by worshiping the golden calf, Moses prayed, "Remember Abraham, Isaac, and Israel, thy servants, to whom thou swarest by thine own self" (Exodus 32:13, KJV). Such prayers invoked God's covenant faithfulness as the basis for divine intervention.

Covenantal Basis of Prayer

Prayer has always been deeply rooted in the concept of covenant. A covenant is a sacred agreement between God and humanity that establishes the terms of the relationship, including blessings, responsibilities, and privileges. In the Old Testament, prayers were heard and answered because they were tethered to these divine agreements. For instance, the Davidic covenant guaranteed the continuation of David's lineage and kingdom. When King Solomon prayed at the dedication of the temple, he appealed to this covenant, saying: "O Lord God of Israel, there is no God like thee, in heaven above, or on earth beneath, who keepest covenant and mercy with thy servants that walk before thee with all their heart" (1 Kings 8:23, KJV). Solomon's prayer acknowledged that God's promises to David formed the basis for His intervention.

The Transition to Jesus' Name

With Christ's advent, a new and superior covenant was inaugurated, fulfilling and surpassing all previous covenants. Jesus is the mediator of the new covenant, sealed with His blood, as described in Hebrews: ***"And to Jesus the mediator of the new covenant, and to the blood of sprinkling, that speaketh better things than that of Abel"*** (Hebrews 12:24, KJV). This covenant granted believers unprecedented access to God through the name of Jesus.

The name of Jesus holds unparalleled power because He is the covenant man who fulfilled every requirement of the law and perfected righteousness before God. Jesus said: "No man cometh unto the Father, but by me" (John 14:6, KJV). Praying in His name, therefore, is not merely a formula but a recognition of His role as our mediator and high priest. The Apostle Paul explains: "For there is one God, and one mediator between God and men, the man Christ Jesus" (1 Timothy 2:5, KJV).

Why Should We Pray in Jesus' Name?

Praying in the name of Jesus acknowledges His covenantal authority and his finished work on the cross. As believers, we approach God not based on our righteousness but Christ's righteousness. His name carries the weight of His sacrifice, His resurrection, and His exaltation to the right hand of God. Philippians states: "Wherefore God also hath highly exalted him and given him a name which is above every name: That at the name of Jesus every knee should bow, of things in heaven, and things in earth, and things under the earth" (Philippians 2:9–10, KJV).

By praying in Jesus' name, we align ourselves with His covenant and access its blessings, including forgiveness, provision, healing, and miracles. This is why the early church consistently emphasized prayer in Jesus' name. Acts record: "To open their eyes and to turn them from darkness to light, and from the power of Satan unto God, that they may receive forgiveness of sins, and inheritance among them which are sanctified by faith that is in me" (Acts 26:18,

KJV). Prayer has always been covenantal; a sacred privilege rooted in God's promises. In the Old Testament, prayers were answered based on the covenants God made with the patriarchs. Today, we pray in the name of Jesus because He is the mediator of a better covenant. His name embodies God's plan for redemption and secures our access to the Father. By understanding the covenantal basis of prayer, we can confidently approach God, knowing that through Jesus, we have a guaranteed connection to His divine counsel and blessings.

CHAPTER 14
Is The Name Of Jesus Absolute?

The assertion that the name of Jesus is absolute needs careful theological and contextual consideration, particularly when examined within the broader biblical narrative and the multifaceted nature of God's provisions. While the name of Jesus holds an undeniably central place in Christian faith—being powerful, exalted, and transformative—an unqualified claim of its exclusivity in all spiritual functions reflects a form of theological reductionism. This perspective does not fully engage with the complexity and dynamism inherent in the operations of God. Scripture presents a divine economy wherein various manifestations, names, and spiritual provisions work collaboratively to fulfill God's redemptive purposes. A more holistic understanding avoids the oversimplification of relying solely on a singular spiritual mechanism, instead inviting a nuanced appreciation for how each divine element complements others within the framework of grace.

To clarify this theological construct, it is helpful to consider the economic principles of **absolute demand** and **relative demand**. Absolute demand refers to something indispensable—an essential element without which the entire system would fail. Relative demand, in contrast, denotes elements that, while not individually sufficient in every context, are necessary for particular functions or circumstances. When viewed theologically, the name of Jesus holds absolute demand in matters concerning salvation and spiritual authority. As affirmed in **Philippians 2:9–10**, God has exalted Jesus and given Him *"the name that is above every name,"* before which every knee shall bow. However, this exaltation does not negate the relative demand of other divine provisions—such as the Holy Spirit, the blood of Jesus, angelic ministry, and covenantal relationships—which are essential for addressing various aspects of spiritual life and fulfilling distinct functions within God's redemptive order.For example, if the name of Jesus alone were wholly sufficient in every context, the promised arrival of the Holy Spirit would appear unnecessary. Yet in **John 16:7,** Jesus declares, *"Nevertheless I tell you the truth: it is expedient for you that I go away; for if I go not away, the Comforter will not come unto you; but if I depart, I will send him unto you."* This statement highlights the essential role of the Holy Spirit, whose functions—such as leading believers into all truth, empowering them, and interceding on their behalf—are not fulfilled merely by invoking the name of Jesus. In this context, the Holy Spirit represents a relative demand within God's redemptive framework. **Romans 8:26** supports this, stating that "the Spirit also helps our infirmities... the Spirit itself maketh intercession for us with groanings which cannot be uttered." The Spirit's distinct work in intercession and empowerment illustrates the multi-layered and cooperative nature of God's divine operations.

Similarly, the blood of Jesus constitutes another essential provision marked by relative demand. While the name of Jesus grants authority and identity to believers, it is the shedding of His blood that secures legal redemption. **Hebrews 9:22** affirms, "Without the shedding of blood, there is no remission of sin." The blood of Christ cleanses, sanctifies, and enacts the covenant between God and humanity (Hebrews 12:24), operating in a spiritual dimension that the name alone does not fully encompass. The name and the blood work in tandem: the former bestows authority, while the latter secures access and purification. Their functions, though distinct, are mutually reinforcing.

Furthermore, the ministry of angels and other spiritual beings introduces yet another dimension of divine orchestration. **Hebrews 1:14** describes angels as "ministering spirits, sent forth to minister for them who shall be heirs of salvation." These beings are not peripheral; they play integral roles in fulfilling God's purposes, occupying functional domains that are not directly fulfilled by either the name of Jesus or the Holy Spirit. Their operation substantiates the concept of relative demand—where specific divine agents are deployed to address particular spiritual or practical needs in accordance with God's sovereign will.

The use of covenantal names throughout Scripture also reinforces this theological framework. God's covenants with Abraham and David imbue their names with enduring spiritual and historical significance. In **Genesis 12:2–3**, Abraham's name becomes a channel of blessing for all nations. Likewise, in **2 Samuel 7:16**, God promises David an everlasting kingdom, thereby linking his name to the messianic lineage. The invocation of such names in prayer or liturgical contexts does not detract from Christ's supremacy; rather, it affirms God's covenantal faithfulness. These names carry relative demand, serving as reminders of divine promises and the continuity of God's work throughout history.

In contemporary Christian practice, some believers appeal to the spiritual authority of covenantal figures—such as spiritual mentors or fathers in the faith—during prayer. Though this practice may be viewed as controversial in some theological circles, it reflects a biblical principle of covenantal representation. Paul, for instance, expresses gratitude through Jesus Christ for the Roman believers, referencing their faith and influence (Romans 1:8). In doing so, he acknowledges the power of names tied to spiritual heritage and responsibility.

This theological exploration in no way diminishes the supremacy of the name of Jesus. It remains foundational—the cornerstone upon which all other spiritual provisions rest. However, framing the name of Jesus as the sole operative mechanism in all spiritual matters risks neglecting the richness and diversity of God's manifold grace. In His infinite wisdom, God has distributed His power and presence across a constellation of spiritual instruments—His name, His blood, His Spirit, angelic ministry, and covenantal relationships. Each of these elements has a distinct function and addresses specific spiritual needs, operating both independently and interdependently.

In conclusion, although the name of Jesus holds absolute authority and is essential for salvation, the full accomplishment of God's redemptive purposes involves a variety of divine provisions that serve relative roles within their specific contexts. Understanding this divine framework enables believers to engage more profoundly with the fullness of God's grace, approaching prayer, worship, and spiritual practice with greater wisdom and effectiveness.

CHAPTER 15
Classical Examples Of Biblical Characters Who Prayed In The Name Of Jesus And Had Their Results

The power of prayer is a central theme in the Christian faith, and the New Testament, particularly after the ascension of Jesus Christ, emphasizes the need to pray in His name. In this regard, prayer in the name of Jesus is not just a tradition; it is a divine instruction with significant spiritual consequences. Throughout the Scriptures, there are many examples of individuals who prayed in Jesus' name and experienced extraordinary results. These instances reveal the immense power and authority vested in the name of Jesus, which believers are encouraged to use in their prayers.

The Early Church's Prayers After Pentecost (Acts 4:23-31)

One of the most profound and early examples of praying in the name of Jesus can be found in the apostles' actions shortly after the Day of Pentecost. In Acts 4:23-31, Peter and John, having been arrested for healing a lame man in the name of Jesus, were released by the Jewish authorities with a stern warning not to speak or teach in Jesus' name. Upon their release, they returned to the company of believers, and together, they prayed to God for boldness in proclaiming the gospel despite the threats against them.

In their prayer, they acknowledged the sovereignty of God, who had created the heavens and the earth. They made a specific appeal: "And now, Lord, behold their threatenings: and grant unto thy servants, that with all boldness they may speak thy word, by stretching forth thine hand to heal; and that signs and wonders may be done by the name of thy holy child Jesus" (Acts 4:29-30, KJV).

This prayer demonstrates the early church's understanding that the name of Jesus was a gateway to boldness, healing, and miraculous signs. The prayer was not just a plea for personal safety but a request for divine intervention to advance the kingdom of God despite opposition. As a result of their prayer, "when they had prayed, the place was shaken where they were assembled; and they were all filled with the Holy Ghost, and they spake the word of God with boldness" (Acts 4:31, KJV). This event highlights the power of praying in Jesus' name, as it resulted in divine confirmation and empowered the apostles to carry out their mission boldly.

The Healing of the Lame Man at the Beautiful Gate (Acts 3:1-10)

A significant and miraculous example of praying in the name of Jesus is the healing of a man who had been lame from birth. In Acts 3:1-10, Peter and John were going to the temple to pray when they encountered a man who had been lame from birth, begging for alms at the Beautiful Gate. Upon seeing him, Peter, filled with the Holy Spirit, addressed the man with a powerful declaration: "Silver and gold have I none; but such as I have give thee: In the name of Jesus Christ of Nazareth, rise and walk" (Acts 3:6, KJV). Peter's words declared the power of Jesus's name. He did not rely on personal wealth, influence, or ability but invoked the authority vested in Jesus' name. Upon this command, the lame man was healed. He leaped up, walking, leaping, and praising God, which drew the attention of the people, who were astonished by the miracle. This event reveals that Jesus' name is mighty in prayer and performing signs and wonders. It is a name that can heal the sick, raise the dead, and transform lives. In this case, Peter used the name of Jesus not just to pray but to speak healing and restoration into the man's life, proving the authority believers have when invoking Jesus' name.

The Prayer of Paul and Silas in Prison (Acts 16:25-34)

Another compelling example of the power of praying in the name of Jesus can be found in Acts 16:25-34 when Paul and Silas were imprisoned in Philippi for casting out a demon from a slave girl who had been making money for her masters by divining. After being severely beaten and placed in stocks, Paul, and Silas, instead of complaining or succumbing to fear, prayed and sang praises to God.

"And at midnight Paul and Silas prayed and sang praises unto God: and the prisoners heard them" (Acts 16:25, KJV). Their prayers and praises were centered on God's power, and using Jesus' name was integral to their communication with the Father. Their prayer was not about self-pity but about invoking the name of Jesus amid their affliction, trusting in His power to deliver them.

At that moment, a miraculous earthquake shook the prison's foundations, breaking open the doors and loosening the prisoners' chains. The jailer, fearing the prisoners had escaped, was about to take his own life, but Paul, calling on the name of Jesus, stopped him. "And they said, believe on the Lord Jesus Christ, and thou shalt be saved, and thy house" (Acts 16:31, KJV). The jailer and his entire household were baptized that night. This example underscores the significance of praying and calling upon the name of Jesus, even in dire circumstances. Their prayer not only resulted in divine deliverance but also brought salvation to an entire household, showing that the name of Jesus is a tool for personal liberation and evangelistic outreach.

The Prayer of Stephen (Acts 7:54-60)

Stephen, the first martyr of the Christian church, gives another powerful example of the effectiveness of invoking Jesus' name in prayer. As the religious leaders were stoning him, Stephen prayed with faith and confidence that came from his relationship with Jesus Christ. As the stones rained upon him, Stephen lifted his eyes to heaven and prayed, "Lord Jesus, receive my spirit" (Acts 7:59, KJV). Stephen's final prayer reveals a deep trust in Jesus. As he confronted death, he called upon the name of the One who had promised eternal life, even in the face of persecution and martyrdom. By invoking Jesus' name in the final moments of his life, Stephen emphasized the profound connection between Jesus and the believer—a relationship that transcends both life and death. His prayer was an act of faith, one that granted him the peace and comfort that only Jesus could provide.

The Prayer of the Apostle Paul for the Ephesians (Ephesians 1:15-23)

In Ephesians 1:15-23, Paul offers a profound prayer for the believers in Ephesus. While not explicitly in Jesus's name, Paul's prayer draws upon Jesus' authority and speaks directly to the benefits believers receive through His work. In his prayer, Paul asks God to grant the Ephesians the spirit of wisdom and revelation in the knowledge of Him.

"That the God of our Lord Jesus Christ, the Father of glory, may give unto you the spirit of wisdom and revelation in the knowledge of him" (Ephesians 1:17, KJV). Paul's prayer acknowledges the authority of the Lord Jesus Christ and calls upon God to bestow His divine wisdom and insight upon the church. Through Jesus, believers could have access to these spiritual blessings, and Paul, in praying, invoked the full authority of Jesus' name and position as the exalted one at the right hand of God. This prayer emphasizes that through Jesus, the believer is endowed with every spiritual blessing in the heavenly realms.

CHAPTER 16
Requirements For Prayer

One of the fundamental aspects of prayer is having a name, as it holds great significance in defining your identity and establishing your connection to the divine. But what identity does this provide? It grants you a rightful place within God's family. It is essential to recognize that God does not hear the prayers of sinners; therefore, the concept of a "sinner's prayer" is not supported by biblical truth. God's name, placed upon you, makes you righteous, and it is this righteousness that qualifies you as a candidate for answered prayer. Scripture affirms that God listens to the prayers of the righteous, not the unrighteous or sinner. Since there is no biblical foundation for the idea of a "sinner's prayer," it is important to understand that only those who are made righteous through Christ are assured that their prayers are heard and answered.

"The LORD is far from the wicked: but he heareth the prayer of the righteous." (Proverbs 15:29, KJV)

One is not considered a member of God's family unless they bear His name. This is not simply a matter of religious observance, but a profound spiritual truth inherent in one's identity as a child of God. The Bible speaks of a "family" both in heaven and on earth—those who are called by God's name:

"For this cause, I bow my knees unto the Father of our Lord Jesus Christ, of whom the whole family in heaven and earth is named." (Ephesians 3:14-15, KJV)

The scripture emphasizes that the name of God registers believers as members of His family. This identity is essential for any prayer to be effective. In the case of Jesus' disciples, God could hear their prayers because they bore God's name. In the book of John, Jesus makes this clear:

"And I have declared unto them thy name and will declare it: that the love wherewith thou hast loved me may be in them, and I in them." (John 17:26, KJV)

This scripture reveals that Jesus imparted God's name to His disciples, granting them access to the Father in a way no one else could claim. By bearing God's name, they could pray effectively and receive answers. The name of God, therefore, is the key to accessing the Father.

Furthermore, the significance of having a name is evident in the Old Testament, where God did not hear the prayers of the children of Israel until He gave them a name. This can be seen in the following scripture:

"If my people, which are called by my name, shall humble themselves, and pray, and seek my face, and turn from their wicked ways; then will I hear from heaven, and will forgive their sin, and will heal their land." (2 Chronicles 7:14, KJV)

In this verse, God clearly affirms that His name defines His people. Only when they are called by His name and humbly turn to Him in prayer will He respond to them. This principle establishes that God's name is not just a title but how He recognizes His people and responds to their prayers. The name of God is paramount in prayer because it signifies a person's identity as a member of God's family. It is not a mere formality but a fundamental aspect of the relationship between believers and the Father. As a child of God, you are identified by His name, and it is through this name that your prayers are heard. Without this name, there is no access to the Father. Thus, the name you bear determines your standing in God's eyes and directly affects the efficacy of your prayers.

CHAPTER 17
The Identity Of Jesus

The identity of Jesus was fundamental to His access to the Father, serving as the foundation through which He fulfilled His redemptive mission and secured salvation for humanity. This concept of identity transcends earthly relevance and extends into the spiritual and heavenly realms, where it functions as a vital credential for divine access. In the same way that individuals on earth require proper authorization to enter restricted spaces, the heavenly order also operates according to the principle of recognized identity. This is powerfully illustrated in Psalm 24:7–10, a passage that symbolically portrays the triumphant entry of Jesus—the King of Glory—into the heavenly gates. The psalmist writes, *"Lift up your heads, O ye gates; and be ye lifted up, ye everlasting doors; and the King of Glory shall come in. Who is this King of Glory? The LORD strong and mighty, the LORD mighty in battle... The LORD of hosts, he is the King of Glory"* (KJV). These verses convey a vivid dialogue between celestial gatekeepers and the returning Christ. The "gates" and "everlasting doors" mentioned in the passage refer to the entry points of the New Jerusalem, the dwelling place of God. As Jesus approaches, the angels stationed as guards ask, "Who is this King of Glory?" This question is not meant to challenge His authority but to affirm His identity before granting Him entry. In response, Jesus affirms His divine status and victorious authority: "The LORD strong and mighty, the LORD mighty in battle." This declaration not only validates His right to enter but also reflects the spiritual principle that access, even in the heavenly realm, is predicated upon identity. It is important to note that this scriptural interaction shows that even Christ, in His glorified state, was subject to the protocol of identification. His declaration, "I am the King of Glory," served as the credential that fulfilled the requirement for entry into the Father's presence.

This heavenly encounter serves as a profound metaphor for believers today. Just as entry into earthly nations and institutions requires proper documentation, spiritual access—whether to divine favor, revelation, or eternal life—requires a clearly affirmed identity. The question "Who are you?" becomes central to one's spiritual advancement. Are you recognized as a child of God, or is your identity undefined or misaligned with the divine order?

The implications of this principle are both spiritual and practical. Without a properly established identity—one that aligns with God's covenant—you may find yourself barred from the very breakthroughs you seek. The name and status of being a child of God carry legal and spiritual weight in both the seen and unseen realms. Jesus' identity as the Son of God and King of Glory granted Him direct access to heaven's throne. Likewise, for believers, it is through the acknowledgment and embodiment of their identity in Christ that they gain access to God's promises and inheritance.

Therefore, the narrative of Psalm 24 does not merely recount a triumphant entry; it underscores a foundational truth: access is granted based on identity. Jesus, by declaring His divine nature, entered into the fullness of God's glory. In the same way, believers who recognize and affirm their spiritual identity as heirs of God's kingdom are positioned to receive the privileges and blessings that accompany that identity. Conversely, a lack of spiritual self-awareness can result in missed opportunities and restricted access.

This truth affirms that identity is not a peripheral concept—it is central to one's relationship with God and to experiencing the fullness of His divine provision.

CHAPTER 18
Foundation Of Names: The Twelve Apostles

The Apostles of the early Church hold a profound and honored place in the divine architecture of Christianity, standing as the foundational pillars upon which the faith was built. Their sacrifices, struggles, and unwavering belief amidst relentless persecution laid the groundwork for the global expansion of the Gospel. According to Scripture, they are described as essential components of the Church's spiritual structure. In the Book of Revelation, the Apostle John recounts a vision in which the names of the twelve apostles are inscribed on the twelve foundations of the New Jerusalem, signifying their monumental role in the establishment of God's eternal kingdom. Revelation 21:14 declares, ***"And the wall of the city had twelve foundations, and in them the names of the twelve apostles of the Lamb."***

Though they were not perfect, Christ chose them to pioneer the Gospel and lead the fledgling Christian community. Their calling was not one of comfort or personal advancement, but one of self-denial, suffering, and martyrdom. Each apostle became a foundation—not only in the spiritual sense but through their very lives, which were often violently taken because of their unwavering testimony of Jesus Christ. Their deaths became a profound testament to their faith and a legacy upon which the Church continues to stand.

Among them, the Apostle Peter stands out as one of the most prominent figures. Often regarded as the rock upon which Jesus said

He would build His Church, Peter's journey of transformation—from denial to bold proclamation—demonstrates the power of grace. In Matthew 16:18, Jesus says, "And I also say unto thee, That thou art Peter, and upon this rock I will build my church; and the gates of hell shall not prevail against it." Though he once faltered, Peter became an unshakable pillar, ultimately embracing martyrdom by crucifixion—tradition holds that he requested to be crucified upside down, deeming himself unworthy to die in the same manner as Christ. His death was a powerful symbol of humility and devotion.

The Apostle Paul, though not one of the original twelve, is also recognized as a foundational figure in the Church's expansion. Once a fierce persecutor of Christians, Paul's radical conversion on the road to Damascus redirected his life toward tireless missionary work and the authorship of much of the New Testament. His ministry extended across the Roman Empire, reaching both Jews and Gentiles. Paul's life was marked by relentless trials—imprisonments, beatings, shipwrecks—and concluded in martyrdom. Tradition holds that he was beheaded in Rome under the reign of Emperor Nero, sealing his legacy as one who was "poured out like a drink offering" (2 Timothy 4:6) for the sake of the Gospel.

James, the brother of John and part of Jesus' inner circle, was the first of the apostles to be martyred. He saw the Transfiguration and Jesus' agony in Gethsemane, experiencing firsthand the depth of Christ's ministry. His zeal for the Kingdom cost him his life under King Herod Agrippa I, as recorded in Acts 12:2: "And he killed James the brother of John with the sword." His early martyrdom set a precedent of courage and faithfulness for those who would follow.

John, the beloved disciple, was the only apostle traditionally believed to have died a natural death, yet his life was not without suffering. He endured exile on the island of Patmos, where he received the apocalyptic visions recorded in the Book of Revelation. His exile—spiritual martyrdom in its own right—was a testament to his endurance. John's long life allowed him to witness the maturation of the early Church, and his theological insights into the love and divinity of Christ remain central to Christian belief.

Andrew, Peter's brother, played a vital role in spreading the Gospel in regions such as Greece and Asia Minor. Tradition tells of his crucifixion on an X-shaped cross in Patras, where he continued preaching for two days before his death. His steadfastness, even in extreme suffering, exemplified the apostolic mission of enduring witness to Christ.

Philip, known for his evangelistic zeal, is believed to have been martyred in Hierapolis, in present-day Turkey. He preached extensively in Greece and Asia Minor, often alongside his sister, a fellow believer. According to tradition, both were crucified, their deaths serving as a powerful testament to the transformative message of the Gospel.

Bartholomew, also known as Nathanael, is remembered for his unwavering faith. He is believed to have been martyred in Armenia, enduring one of the most brutal deaths—flayed alive and then beheaded. His sacrifice embodies the extreme cost of discipleship and the depth of his commitment to Christ.

Thomas, often remembered for doubting the resurrection, later became a bold and tireless evangelist. He is traditionally credited with bringing the Gospel as far as India, where he established Christian communities. He paid the ultimate price for his faith, being speared to death. Thomas' legacy stands as a powerful symbol of transformation and missionary zeal.

Matthew, once a tax collector, left his wealth and status to follow Jesus. His Gospel account remains one of the pillars of the New Testament. Tradition holds that he ministered in Ethiopia and was martyred there. Though the details of his death are uncertain, his life and writings left an indelible mark on Christian history.

These apostles are far more than distant historical figures; they are the very foundation upon which the Church is built. Their courage, devotion, and sacrifice echo through the ages, bearing witness to their faith in Christ even unto death. Revelation 21:14 confirms their eternal place in God's kingdom: "And the wall of the city had twelve foundations, and in them the names of the twelve apostles of the Lamb." Their names inscribed on the foundations of the New Jerusalem are not only a testament to their legacy but also a divine affirmation of their role in the unfolding of God's redemptive plan. Through their lives and deaths, they became the living stones upon which Christ's Church stands—unshakable, enduring, and eternally rooted in the truth of the Gospel.

CHAPTER 19
Jesus Christ: The Solid Foundation For Building God's People

In 1 Corinthians 3:11, the Apostle Paul asserts, ***"For other foundation can no man lay than that is laid, which is Jesus Christ."*** This declaration affirms that Jesus Christ constitutes the ultimate and exclusive foundation upon which the Church must be established. Every church leader—whether prophet, pastor, teacher, apostle, or evangelist—bears the responsibility of building the community of believers upon this firm, immutable foundation. Departing from Christ as the foundation risks constructing a structure that lacks stability and permanence. The foundation that Christ provides is eternal, and only through adherence to His truth can the Church withstand trials across all ages.

This foundational principle is further emphasized in Matthew 16:13-18, where Jesus questions His disciples about His identity: ***"Whom do men say that I, the Son of man, am?"*** Peter responds with divinely inspired insight, declaring, "Thou art the Christ, the Son of the living God." Jesus affirms Peter's confession, stating, "Blessed art thou, Simon Barjona: for flesh and blood hath not revealed it unto thee, but my Father which is in heaven. And I say also unto thee, That thou art Peter, and upon this rock I will build my church; and the gates of hell shall not prevail against it."

In this passage, the "rock" upon which the Church is built refers to the divine revelation of Christ's messianic identity. This is not merely intellectual assent but a profound, God-given truth. Jesus' proclamation highlights that the Church's establishment depends on the recognition and acceptance of His person and redemptive mission. Foundations laid on any other basis are fundamentally unstable.

Consequently, ministers must critically evaluate the foundation upon which they instruct and nurture their congregations. Are believers being grounded in the teachings of Christ Himself, or are they inadvertently encouraged to follow human leaders—pastors, founders, or prophets? The risk of elevating human philosophies or teachings above the doctrine of Christ must be conscientiously avoided.

In contemporary Christian practice, it is common to encounter influential teachers and authors whose insights enrich the faith community. While such contributions may be valuable, they must not supplant the primacy of Christ's teaching. Paul's admonition in 1 Corinthians 3:10 offers a solemn warning:

"According to the grace of God which is given unto me, as a wise master builder, I have laid the foundation, and another buildeth thereon. But let every man take heed how he buildeth thereupon."

This exhortation underscores the imperative that all teaching and ministry be firmly anchored in the foundation of Jesus Christ. Any deviation threatens the spiritual integrity and longevity of the Church.

Ministers must also resist the temptation to focus attention on their own work, writings, or ideas rather than on Christ. While ministerial contributions can aid spiritual growth, they must always direct believers back to the central truth of the Gospel. The faith of the congregation must be rooted in Christ alone, not in the opinions or doctrines of human leaders. Throughout Christian history, numerous churches and movements have emerged; however, those that neglected to uphold Christ as their central foundation eventually diminished. Their teachings rested on fleeting and unstable grounds, lacking the permanence found in the enduring truth of Jesus Christ. Conversely, ministries that consistently center their message on Christ's Gospel exhibit enduring impact and vitality. The imperative to build on Christ's foundation is echoed in Jesus' parable of the wise and foolish builders (Matthew 7:24-25):

"Therefore whosoever heareth these sayings of mine, and doeth them, I will liken him unto a wise man, which built his house upon a rock: And the rain descended, and the floods came, and the winds blew, and beat upon that house; and it fell not: for it was founded upon a rock."

This metaphor reinforces the certainty and security that arise from building one's life and faith community on the solid foundation of Christ's teachings.

In conclusion, those who minister the Gospel bear a solemn responsibility to ensure that Jesus Christ remains the unshakable foundation of the Church. Only in Him can believers find lasting security, stability, and hope. It is imperative that ministry efforts focus on grounding God's people in Christ, thereby enabling them to stand firm in their faith and reflect His glory throughout their lives.

CHAPTER 20
The Attributes Of God

Throughout Scripture, God discloses His character, nature, and divine authority through a multitude of names. These names are not merely descriptive labels; they embody profound theological truths and serve as pathways for believers to engage with God according to their circumstances and needs. Each name unveils a distinct dimension of God's relationship with His people. Among these, the title "Lord" stands out for its association with divine sovereignty and His role as a defender and deliverer in times of conflict.

1. The Name "Lord" – Divine Warrior and Defender

The designation "Lord" (Hebrew: *YHWH*, often rendered\ *Adonai*) signifies God's supreme authority and dominion. It is frequently used in the context of spiritual warfare and divine intervention. In Exodus 14:14, the Israelites found themselves in a desperate situation, trapped between the Red Sea and the pursuing Egyptian army. In response to their plight, God intervened on their behalf, assuring them of His protection and victory:

> *"The LORD shall fight for you, and ye shall hold your peace." (Exodus 14:14, KJV)*

This passage underscores the theological theme of God as a warrior who actively defends His people. The notion is reinforced in Exodus 15:3:

> *"The LORD is a man of war: the LORD is His name." (Exodus 15:3, KJV)*

These verses collectively affirm God's role as the leader of heavenly armies, demonstrating His ability to confront and overcome any opposition on behalf of His people.

2. Jehovah Nissi – The Lord is My Banner

The name *Jehovah Nissi* originates in the narrative of Exodus 17, where Israel, under Moses' leadership, defeated the Amalekites. Following this victory, Moses constructed an altar and named it Jehovah Nissi, meaning "The Lord is My Banner":

> ***"And Moses built an altar, and called the name of it Jehovah-Nissi." (Exodus 17:15, KJV)***

This title symbolizes God's protective leadership and His role as the standard around which His people rally during times of adversity. The imagery of a banner implies both identity and victory, indicating that the Lord's presence is the decisive factor in overcoming life's battles—spiritual, emotional, or physical.

3. El Shaddai – The All-Sufficient God

El Shaddai, often translated as "God Almighty" or "The All-Sufficient One," communicates God's absolute sufficiency and omnipotence. This name first appears in Genesis 17:1, when God establishes His covenant with Abraham:

> ***"And when Abram was ninety years old and nine, the LORD appeared to Abram, and said unto him, I am the Almighty God; walk before me, and be thou perfect." (Genesis 17:1, KJV)***

El Shaddai emphasizes God's ability to supply every need of His people. Whether in times of scarcity, weakness, or uncertainty, He is fully capable of sustaining and fulfilling His promises. This name reassures believers of God's inexhaustible resources and unwavering faithfulness.

4. Jehovah Jireh – The Lord Will Provide

The name *Jehovah Jireh*, meaning "The Lord Will Provide," is derived from the account of Abraham's willingness to offer Isaac as a sacrifice. In response to Abraham's obedience and faith, God intervened by providing a ram as a substitute. In recognition of this divine provision, Abraham named the place *Jehovah Jireh*.

> ***"And Abraham called the name of that place Jehovah-Jireh: as it is said to this day, In the mount of the LORD it shall be seen." (Genesis 22:14, KJV)***

This divine title assures believers of God's provision in critical moments. Jehovah Jireh extends beyond material needs, encompassing emotional support, spiritual guidance, and prompt interventions. His provision is both sufficient and purposeful, aligned with His perfect will and timing.

5. Jehovah Rapha – The Lord Who Heals

Jehovah Rapha, meaning "The Lord Who Heals," speaks to God's restorative nature. In Exodus 15:26, following the Israelites' encounter with the bitter waters of Marah, God declared Himself their healer:

> ***"If thou wilt diligently hearken to the voice of the LORD thy God, and wilt do that which is right in his sight... I will put none of these diseases upon thee... for I am the LORD that healeth thee." (Exodus 15:26, KJV)***

This name encompasses both physical and spiritual healing. It affirms that God's capacity to heal is integral to His nature. Whether the affliction is bodily, emotional, or spiritual, believers are invited to trust in Jehovah Rapha for complete restoration and wholeness.

6. Jehovah Tsidkenu – The Lord Our Righteousness

The name *Jehovah Tsidkenu*, translated "The Lord Our Righteousness," is introduced in Jeremiah 23:6 during a prophetic vision concerning the Messianic reign:

> ***"In his days Judah shall be saved, and Israel shall dwell safely: and this is his name whereby he shall be called, The LORD Our Righteousness." (Jeremiah 23:6, KJV)***

This title emphasizes that righteousness is not earned through human effort but granted through divine grace. It points ultimately to the redemptive work of Jesus Christ, who embodies and imparts righteousness to those who believe. Through Him, believers are justified and reconciled to God.

7. Jehovah Shalom – The Lord is Peace

Jehovah Shalom, meaning "The Lord is Peace," was declared by Gideon after a divine encounter during a period of national oppression. Overwhelmed by fear, Gideon was comforted by God's promise of peace, prompting him to build an altar:

> ***"Then Gideon built an altar there unto the LORD and called it Jehovah-shalom." (Judges 6:24, KJV)***

This name reveals God as the source of true peace—peace that surpasses human understanding and is undisturbed by external turmoil. Jehovah Shalom offers inner tranquility, emotional stability, and spiritual calmness, even amidst life's most chaotic circumstances.

The names of God, as revealed in Scripture, are deeply theological and convey critical aspects of His character, covenantal faithfulness, and divine intervention. Whether believers seek deliverance, provision, healing, righteousness, or peace, each divine name provides a specific avenue through which they can approach God with confidence. Engaging with these names in prayer fosters a deeper understanding of His nature and invites His active presence into every area of life. Calling upon the name of the Lord is more than a religious act—it is a declaration of trust in the fullness of who God is.

www.ingramcontent.com/pod-product-compliance
Lightning Source LLC
Chambersburg PA
CBHW052107070526
44584CB00017B/2371